MAKING MORAL DECISIONS SUPPORT EDITION

A textbook for Intermediate 1 and 2
Scottish Qualifications Authority
National Qualifications
in
Religious, Moral & Philosophical Studies

Joe Walker

A MEMBER OF THE HODDER HEADLINE GROUP

Photo Acknowledgements

The publishers would like to thank the following individuals, institutions and companies for permission to reproduce photographs in this book. Every effort has been made to trace ownership of copyright. The publishers would be happy to make arrangements with any copyright holder whom it has not been possible to contact.

Associated Press pages 66, 68, 90; Frank Capri page 34; Bruce Coleman page 143; Corbis page 104; Bettinann/Corbis page 10, 97; Jeremy Hornet/Corbis page 7; Frank Lane Picture Agency/Corbis page 137; Ed Kashi/Corbis page 127; Paplin/Corbis page 144; Reuters Newmedia Inc./Corbis pages 2, 43, 52; Richard Duszczak page 116; copyright Warner Bros. Paramount Pictures. The Ronald Grant Archive page 84; Hodder & Stoughton page 83; Hulton Archive photos page 119; Mary Evans Picture Library page 8; PA Photos pages 17, 30, 35, 46, 92, 99, 105, 129, 152; Graham Burns/Photofusion page 81; Equal Opportunities Commission 118; Crispin Hughes/Photofusion page 121; Nicky Johnston/Photofusion page 51; Warren Powell/ Photofusion page 114; Joseph Sohm/ChromoSohm Inc page 112; Helen Stone/Photofusion page 61; Sam Tanner/Photofusion pages 21, 37; Mike Wilce/Photofusion page 76; Popperfoto/Reuters page 106; copyright John Reilly page 6; Alex Bartel/Science Photo Library page 153; Simon Fraser/Science Photo Library page 150; Francis Leroy, Biocosmos/Science Photo Library page 13; Michelle Del Gurcio, Custom Medical Stock Photo/Science Photo Library page 27; Petit Format/Nestle/Science Photo Library page 15; Chris Priest/Science Photo Library page 29; Ed Young/Science Photo Library page 134; Scottish Executive 126; Michael Boyd/Scottish News Agency page 75; SMN Archive page 132; Stuart Conway 139; UN DPI page 90; Graham White page 142.

The "Three Faces" poster (p 77) forms part of an ongoing and award-winning CARE programme (Co-ordinated Action on Racism in Edinburgh) which has been developed by the Black & Minority Ethnic Communities Safety Group (BMECSG). The BMECSG is a Working Group of the Edinburgh Community Safety Partnership which is supported by the Community Safety Unit of the City of Edinburgh Council. Tel: 0131 469 3871

The illustration was drawn by Richard Duszczak

Orders: please contact Bookpoint Ltd, 130 Milton Park, Abingdon, Oxon OX14 4SB. Telephone: (44) 01235 827720. Fax: (44) 01235 400454. Lines are open from 9.00–5.00, Monday to Saturday, with a 24 hour message answering service. You can also order through our website www.hoddereducation.co.uk

British Library Cataloguing in Publication Data
A catalogue record for this title is available from the British Library

ISBN-10: 0 340 84627 5
ISBN-13: 978 0 340 84627 8

Published by Hodder Gibson, 2a Christie Street, Paisley PA1 1NB.
Tel: 0141 848 1609; Fax: 0141 889 6315; email: hoddergibson@hodder.co.uk
First published 2002
Impression number 10 9 8 7 6 5 4 3
Year 2008 2007 2006

Cover photo from Peter Samuels/Corbis
Typeset by Dorchester Typesetting Group Limited, Dorchester, Dorset DT1 1UA
Printed in Great Britain for Hodder Gibson, 2a Christie Street, Paisley, PA1 1NB, Scotland, UK by Martins the Printers, Berwick upon Tweed.

Acknowledgements

Thanks again to Lorna and David for their patience during this work. Simplifying a text is no less time-consuming and fraught an exercise than writing from scratch.

Thanks to the many colleagues, particularly those in the world of Support for Learning, who provided helpful comment and guidance about language level, presentation style and the nature of tasks which are appropriate.

About the Author

Joe Walker is Head of Religious, Moral and Philosophical Studies at Liberton High School in Edinburgh. He was Secretary of ATRES for four years. He was part of the original Central Support Group during the development of Standard Grade Religious Studies and has marked Standard Grade since its inception. He was, for four years, a member of the Scottish Examination Board and then Scottish Qualifications Authority, Religious Studies Panel. As part of this work, he has been responsible for vetting, setting, moderating and many other tasks for the SQA. He is the writer of a range of support materials and NAB items for the HSDU, then SQA, at all levels, including Advanced Higher Bioethics. He was Development Officer for RME for the City of Edinburgh Council. His other books with Hodder & Stoughton are: *Our World: Religion and Environment* (0340 605499); *Their World: Religion and Animal Issues* (0340 721162); *World Issues: Religion and Morality* [with Jim Green] (0340 781815); *Environmental Ethics* (0340 757701).

To the Teacher

The original *Making Moral Decisions* textbook is intended as a comprehensive working of all of the areas of the Scottish Qualifications Authority's Making Moral Decisions Unit at Intermediate 1 and 2. However, practising teachers appreciate that even if they are officially running a bi-level class, it may often be tri-level at the very least.

This book is intended to be used alongside *Making Moral Decisions*. It includes the full range of optional issues. Moreover, the text has been completely rewritten to accommodate lower levels of reading and comprehension. The tasks have also been revised to give greater direction to the less able. Nevertheless, the same format in *Making Moral Decisions* is followed throughout. This should enable pupils of a wider ability range to work through the same learning process in parallel. The closeness of the set activities should mean that the teacher is not given another burdensome layer of marking. Many pupils will have the necessary ability to understand and explore the important issues in this course, but may be hampered by reading and basic comprehension. This support edition is an attempt to remedy this possibility, thereby opening up these fascinating and thought-provoking issues to all pupils.

As in the original edition, teachers should be satisfied that they are working from the most recent SQA arrangements documents with respect to course content and assessment procedures.

Contact: mobyjoe1uk@yahoo.co.uk

Contents

1 Making moral decisions

Case Study

A word from the author

It's a cold, dark miserable morning. I don't really feel like going to school. But I always go. Why?

- The **consequences** of not going aren't good. Other teachers will have to look after my classes. The Head Teacher might argue with me if I'm off too much. I need the job, I need the money.
- I'd feel **guilty** lying in my bed knowing other people were working hard.
- The '**rules**' of the job say I should always try to get to work. If I don't follow them, why should anyone else?
- If I skive, I set a bad **example** to others.
- I quite like my work (most of the time).
- If you want to be **reliable** you should go to work when you can. This makes everyone's life easier!

Discussion Point

Which of these reasons do you think is the best one for going to school? Why?

How moral decisions are made

Good reasons

If your teacher asked you to throw a friend's mobile phone out of the window, you would probably say 'no' (I hope! But why have a mobile in class anyway?)

Right and wrong isn't easy – take killing as an example. Is there any difference between these three ways of killing?

- Killing an enemy in war.
- Stabbing someone in the street because you don't like their face.
- Giving a dying person drugs to end their life.

CONSCIENCE

Some people think right and wrong is 'in your head'. This is called your **conscience**. You just know. When the teacher asked you to chuck your friend's mobile out of the window you somehow just knew that this was wrong. You didn't have to think about it. Some people think things are right if doing them makes them feel good. But maybe some people enjoy killing others. Does that make it right? Anyway, where does your conscience come from?

figure 1.1 *A courtroom scene. Society makes rules which we have to live by. The courts are there to punish those who break the rules*

RULES

Some people don't think about right and wrong, they just follow the rules. These can be school rules, house rules or national rules. These rules are sometimes made into laws. Who makes these rules? Should we just follow them without thinking about them? Once something is 'the Law' is it unbreakable? Or should we break the law when we think it's wrong?

TRADITIONS

Some things have just 'always been that way'. There are ways of behaving that are **traditional.** We follow these rules because everyone else does. Is that right?

BORN BAD?

- Are people born more likely to do bad things or do they get that way as they get older?
- Here's an interesting idea. What do you think of it?
  'Right' = whatever brings rewards (or makes you happy).
  'Wrong' = whatever brings punishment (or makes you unhappy). We learn which is which when we are children.
- Or is doing the right thing just what helps us to **survive**?

Are some things 'always wrong'?

Ask your parents if they think people are more selfish now than they were in their day.

ABSOLUTE AND RELATIVE MORALITY

Absolute morality = there are some things which are always right or wrong. This is true no matter what the situation is. So killing is wrong whatever the reason.

Relative morality = what's right and wrong depends on the situation. Sometimes it is right to take a life.

ARE THINGS 'GETTING WORSE'?

Older people sometimes say this. They sometimes think that young people don't care about their behaviour the way people did in the past. Is that true? Are people nicer or nastier now?

WHAT'S THE POINT?

You might never have to cope with some of the things you will see in this book. So, why bother?

- It will help you to work out what you think about a lot of different things.
- You will get to hear other people's views.
- It helps you to work out what part you play in the world today.
- It will help you to grow up!

Read this story and ask yourself:

- What wrong things were done here?
- Who was to blame?
- How should the killers be punished?

CASE STUDY

Mark Ayton (19) was killed in Balerno, Edinburgh after a fight. Some of those involved had been drinking.

Mark's face was kicked so hard it left bootlace marks. Mark was Scottish, but had an English accent. This was because he'd lived in England. His father thought this was maybe why he was attacked.

The killers were all local boys, and all 16 years old. They came from well-off families. Their dads were a policeman, a managing director and a senior civil servant.

A newspaper reported, 'Mark's death was caused by a few moments of pointless violence. There's no explanation for it'.

MORAL STANCES

MIX AND MATCH

When you make a decision about right and wrong you usually know why you have made one choice and not another. But behind your decision there might be a whole way of thinking. We can call this a viewpoint, or a **moral stance**. This might be your own moral stance. You might share it with other people. Sometimes this stance is strong – it affects every decision you make. Sometimes it is weak – it just pushes you in one direction. In RMPS you have to know about two moral stances at Intermediate 1 level and three at Intermediate 2. Maybe one of these will be yours!

Have you got a moral stance?

RELIGIOUS AUTHORITY: CHRISTIANITY

This was started by **Jesus**. Christians think that Jesus is the Son of God. But he is God himself too. Jesus was Jewish. He followed Jewish teachings but sometimes did his own thing with them. He sometimes added on to them too. After his death and resurrection, the first Christians tried to put his teachings into practice. They wrote things down so that no one would forget. They added this to the Jewish holy books. This is now called the Christian Bible. Christians today try to work out what the Bible teaches about modern things. This isn't always easy, because times have changed.

- **The Bible:** Many Christians believe that the Bible is completely true. God gave it to humans so it must all be right. You just follow what it teaches. Some other Christians say that the Bible wasn't written to cope with the problems of the 21st century. You have to try to make sense of it in the modern world. Some Christians even think that you just use the Bible as a starting point. It has some general rules which you can apply to modern problems. After that, it is up to you.
- **Tradition:** After Jesus, the Christian churches worked out their own meanings of Jesus' teachings. They passed these meanings down to their followers. These traditions are still followed.
- **Authority:** Christian leaders, past and present, help ordinary Christians to make moral decisions. For Roman Catholics there is the Pope. For the Church of Scotland, a yearly meeting – called the General Assembly – helps ordinary Christians find out what's right and wrong.
- **Prayer and direct revelation:** Many Christians believe that God tells them directly what's right and wrong. They pray and their prayers are answered. They have to check carefully what they think God is telling them. This is so they get it right. They will check what they think God is telling them with the Bible and other Christians, for example.

Some Christian ideas about right and wrong (moral principles)

- Love one another.
- Be kind to everyone.
- Look after the weak.
- Think of others before you think of yourself.
- Always be fair.
- Don't be hard on people – God can do that if it is necessary.
- Make the world the kind of place God would want it to be.

figure 1.2 *A contemporary depiction of Jesus Christ*

RELIGIOUS AUTHORITY: ISLAM

This religion was started by the Prophet Muhammed. Muslims believe that God gave Muhammed a holy book. This is the Qur'an. These are the actual words of Allah (God). Muhammed taught that there is only one God. Allah knows everything and sees everything. When the Muslim dies he will have to face Allah. Allah will know how good or bad each person has been. This means that all moral decisions made by Muslims are seen by Allah. But there is no excuse, Muslims know what is right and wrong. They get this from:

- **The Qur'an:** These are the actual words of Allah. Muslims believe it has all the teachings in it you need to live a good life. But things in it can be understood in different ways. This can mean different Muslims make different decisions – all based on the same Qur'an.
- **The Sunnah:** During his life, Muhammed set examples for others to follow. Sometimes this was by what he did. Sometimes it was by what Muhammed said. Because Muslims think Muhammed was specially chosen by Allah they follow his example carefully. But even his example is not as important as the teachings in the Qur'an.

- **The Shariah**: Through the years, Muslim teachers have made up laws. These laws are based on the Qur'an and Sunnah. These laws help ordinary Muslims in their everyday lives.
- **Culture and Tradition**: As Muslims moved around the world, they **mixed** their beliefs and actions with the people they met. So even though the important teachings are the same, the way of understanding them might be different, depending on where you live.
- **Authority**: Muslim teachers, like the Imam in the mosque, help ordinary Muslims to know what is right and wrong.
- **Experience**: Some Muslims, like the Sufis, believe that Allah still speaks directly to people today.

Some Muslim ideas about right and wrong (Muslim moral principles)

- If something helps people it is good. If it harms them it is bad.
- If you live your life trying to please Allah you will live a good life.

figure 1.3 *A muslim child studying the Qu'ran*

- Allah has shown humans how to be good.
- The people in the community (Ummah) of Islam should help each other.
- Being humble, not showing off, controlling yourself, telling the truth and keeping your promises are all important.

EGOISM

This is not a religion, but a way of thinking. Sometimes it is called a moral philosophy – which is another way of saying a way of thinking! A Greek called Epicurus (341–270 BCE) said that what brought you pleasure was right. He thought every pleasure was linked to your 'belly'! Egoists think that what is right is best for you. But you have to be careful – you can have too much of a good thing. One Mars bar might be nice, but 100 would not be 100 times better. It would make you sick! A man called Friedrich Nietzsche (1844–1900) said you have to control your own life. If you don't you won't be happy. Thomas Hobbes (1588–1679) said that the only way to be happy was to be selfish. What was right was what pleased you most. You might even have to join together with others to make sure your own selfishness was satisfied! How do Egoists make decisions about right and wrong?

figure 1.4 *Friedrich Nietzsche*

- **Themselves!** You might read books about right and wrong and listen to teachers, but what is right and wrong is what works best for you. You make your moral decisions depending on the situation at the time. You have to make sure that what you're doing is **best for you.** That is not always easy! You never know how something will work out!

Some Egoist ideas about right and wrong (Egoist moral principles)

- All your decisions should be based on what is best for you.
- You work out each situation at the time and decide what to do about it.
- You might still follow some rules. For example, the rule 'do not kill' is always good for the Egoist because it keeps him alive.
- You have to weigh up the benefits of one action now, thinking about any problems it might cause you in the future.
- You can even do things for other people – if it is good for you in the end!

UTILITARIANISM

This is not a religion either. It is another way of thinking (moral philosophy). Jeremy Bentham (1748–1832), whose stuffed body is in a glass box for all to see in University College, London, said that doing what's right must be good for most people (the majority). It must cause as little unhappiness for others as possible. He called this Utility.

John Stuart Mill (1806–1873) also said that what right is what best for most people. This also causes least harm to most people. So when you are deciding what is right and wrong, this is what you do if you are a Utilitarian. If it produces the most pleasure for most people then it is right, if it doesn't it is wrong. There are different kinds of Utilitarianism:

- **Rule Utilitarianism:** Some rules will always be more likely to make most people happy. So you don't need to judge each situation on its own. For example, the rule 'do not kill' is usually best for most people! The rule decides what you will do.

- **Act Utilitarianism:** If what you are going to do will probably give most people pleasure, then it is right. What might happen decides what you will do.

The big problem for the Utilitarian is how you know what you are doing now will be best for most people. What about the effects it might have in the future? How do you know that what you think is pleasure is nice? Someone else might hate it!

Some Utilitarian ideas about right and wrong (Utilitarian moral principles)

- What you do should bring the greatest happiness for most people.
- You have to judge this for yourself. Your government might do it too.
- You cannot ignore the needs of others. This could make everyone unhappy.
- You can be selfish or selfless. It depends on what is best for most people!
- Everyone is equal.

figure 1.5 *John Stuart Mill*

APPLYING YOUR MORAL STANCE

Some people will stick very closely to their moral stance. Some will be more flexible. Some people will mix them up. You might be a Christian Utilitarian, but probably not a Christian Egoist!

Humans are complicated. The things you will study in this book are too.

Making moral decisions is not easy.

KEY WORDS

Conscience – What you think or feel is right 'in your head'.

Laws – Ways of showing what a society thinks is right or wrong.

Moral stance – A way of thinking which helps you make moral decisions.

Traditional – When something has been done 'that way' for a long time.

ACTIVITIES

Knowledge & Understanding

1. Give **three** reasons why you came to school this morning.
2. Copy and match up the following words and their explanations:
   Words: Consequences, Guilty, Rules, Example, Reliable
   Explanations
   - When you feel bad about something you have done.
   - Another word for codes of conduct.
   - When you do something which others might copy.
   - When people know they can depend on you.
   - When one thing follows another.
3. Give **three** reasons why someone might refuse to take off their clothes and dance on the table.
4. Give **two** reasons why someone might throw their friend's mobile phone out of the window if their teacher asked them to.
5. Do you think all ways of killing are equally wrong? Explain your answer in at least 30 words.
6. Write down **two** rules you think are fair, and **two** rules you think are unfair.
7. Should we always obey the law? Give **one** reason for your answer in no less than 20 words.
8. Can you think of anything people do because it is 'traditional'?
9. Do you think people are born bad? Give a reason for your answer in no less than 20 words.
10. In your own words, explain the difference between absolute and relative morality.

11 Do you think young people today are not as bothered about right and wrong as their parents were when they were young?

12 In your own words answer the questions on page 4 about the Mark Ayton story.

13 Why do you think so many people were shocked by the killing of Mark Ayton? List as many reasons as you can.

Extension work

There are some ideas about right and wrong which people all over the world seem to share. To show this, try the following.

a Imagine you have become the President of a United World following a war in which millions have been killed. In pairs, make a list of seven laws you would make to keep your new society safe and stable.

b Now get together with another pair, and in fours make a new list of laws based on the ones you have in common.

c Now get together with another group of four and do the same for your group of eight.

2 MEDICAL ETHICS

THE TREATMENT OF EMBRYOS

CASE STUDY

Alan and Louise Masterton had a daughter. In July 1999 she died. They want to have another baby, but they want to make sure it's a girl. They think they can do this by getting scientists to help them. This is called *genetic technology*.

At the moment you can only get help to choose the sex of your child for one reason. If your family has an illness which is passed on to boys, you can choose to have a girl. Or the other way round.

This is all watched over by an organisation called the Human Fertilisation and Embryology Authority (HFEA). They don't think the Mastertons want a girl for the right reason so they're not letting the scientists help them. Alan and Louise are taking the HFEA to court.

They both go to St Aidan's Church of Scotland in Broughty Ferry. They say that choosing the sex of their child is not 'playing God'. It is just a choice, the same as using a contraceptive is choosing not to have children.

figure 2.1 *The sperm and ovum at the moment of conception*

WHEN DOES LIFE BEGIN?

When a man and woman have sex, the **sperm** and **egg** join. This is called **fertilisation** or **conception**. The joined egg and sperm (**blastocyte/pre-embryo**) contain chemical 'information'. This information is called **DNA**. It decides lots of things, like the colour of your eyes, and what illnesses you might have.

After 14 days, this pre-embryo starts to form the different cells which will make different parts of your body. It is now called an embryo. Some say this is when 'you' really begin. Others say you begin:

- Six days after fertilisation when the pre-embryo sticks to the wall of the woman's uterus (implantation).
- At 54 days, when your brain starts working (scientists have recorded some brain waves at 40 days).
- When you can feel pain, though scientists disagree about when this is.
- When the growing child can survive on its own outside the woman's body.
- From the moment you're born.

Some people also think that life starts at the moment of conception. From this point all the information needed to make you is there. Now you just grow bigger.

Some religious people think this is when you get a soul (ensoulment). People who are not religious might also say this is when you begin. This is because from the moment of conception you are becoming what you will be when you're older. They would say you are a **potential person**.

DISCUSSION POINT

When do you think life begins?

WHY THIS MATTERS

When your life begins is important. When you are a person you should have rights. Scientists use **pre-embryos** to do tests (research). In the UK you can only use a pre-embryo for tests until it is 14 days old. These embryos come from women who don't want them. Why wouldn't you?

When some people are trying for a baby they get medical help (IVF – *in vitro* fertilisation). The woman is given drugs. These make her produce a lot of eggs at once. They take the eggs out of the woman. The doctors then add sperm to the eggs to produce an embryo. They then choose the 'best' embryos and put them back into the woman. This is done in a glass dish in the laboratory – so the babies get called 'test-tube babies'.

The ones the scientists don't use (spare embryos) can be used for research along with embryos specially made for research:

1 **Gene therapy:** Sometimes people are born with certain illnesses. These are 'genetic'. If you can fix them when the embryo is developing, then the person won't get the illness. But you have to know what the problem is and how to fix it. Using spare embryos for tests might help you do this. Some people think scientists might use these tests to try out ways to 'improve' people. The scientists can decide how you will turn out by changing your genetic information. So you could choose what your child will be like (designer babies).
2 **Applied research:** Sometimes tests are done on embryos to help people work out why genetic problems happen. This may help scientists find out why some people cannot have babies.
3 **Pure research:** Sometimes the scientists don't know what good things might come from their work. They might accidentally find a cure for something.

The HFEA is in charge of all these tests. It has rules which the scientists have to stick to. HFEA says that they're *trying to make sure that scientists can learn useful things. But they shouldn't be taking advantage of people at a difficult time, or when they can't speak for themselves.*

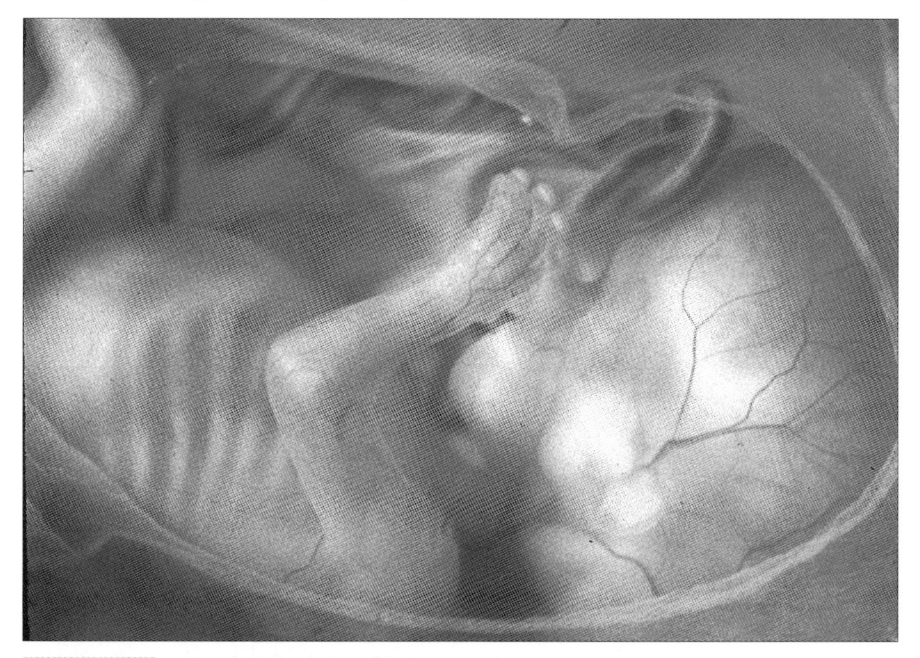

figure 2.2 *Embryonic development*

RESEARCH OR NOT – THE ARGUMENTS

Some people think that using any person for research, even a one day-old pre-embryo is wrong. Why?

- The pre-embryo cannot tell us what it wants. Because of this, we're taking advantage of it.
- It is wrong to use a pre-embryo and then just throw it away.
- Fiddling about with the pre-embryo's information is like 'playing God'.
- If you get rid of what you *don't like* in a pre-embryo, how do you decide what that is? When you say that's a good thing and that isn't, you end up choosing the future. That is worrying.
- This could mean that you might end up 'creating' just beautiful or intelligent people (eugenics).
- Maybe there are other ways to do the research, for example, with adult stem cells or umbilical cords.

Most scientists know about these problems. But they think it would be just as wrong not to use our abilities for good because:

- Using pre-embryos might be the *only* way to find out some things.
- If you can put something right you should. Does anyone really want a child born with a serious disability?
- Every time we take a pill we 'play God'.
- Stopping people having illnesses later in life is not the same as making 'designer babies'.
- This scientific work is strictly controlled.
- The pre-embryo is *not a person*. We don't control the way eggs and sperm are treated – so what is the difference once they're joined?

DISCUSSION POINT

Do you think it is right to use pre-embryos for scientific research?

THE VALUE OF LIFE

So, one of the big questions here is 'When does life begin?'. The other is, 'How valuable is life?' There are two important views here.

1 Life is **sacred** (the **sanctity of life** argument). This is usually a religious view, but not always. Sometimes this means that life is God's gift.

So, we should treat life with care right from the start (whenever that is). We should not mess about with it. God (or 'nature') makes everyone the way he (it) wants to. It is not up to us to decide what is good and what is bad. Instead of getting rid of things we don't like in people, we should learn to live with them.

Some people think that life is sacred, but sometimes we have to take a life for a good reason. If tests on one pre-embryo can help thousands of people for years to come, then maybe we should do the tests. The pre-embryo is 'sacrificed' for a good cause.

figure 2.3 *Pro-life protestors*

Do you think the sanctity of life argument or the quality of life argument is best?

2 The **quality of life** argument. Some people think life is only worth living when we are conscious, thinking people. The pre-embryo doesn't have proper consciousness, so it is not completely 'alive'.Therefore, we can use it for research. If that can make people's lives better then it must be good. If using the pre-embryo doesn't really harm it (because there's nothing to feel harm), then why not?

FACTS AND FIGURES

◆ A woman has a limited supply of eggs. Men can make new sperm all of their lives.

◆ Over 3000 illnesses are caused by faulty genetic information. About one in 100 babies has an illness caused by just one gene gone wrong.

◆ Cloning is another scientific idea. If it works with people you could make a new you out of every cell in your body!

MORAL RESPONSES

CHRISTIANITY

Christians say that life is sacred. Only God should take it (Job 1:21). Jesus was a person at the moment of conception, so everyone else must be too. God even knows who you are when you're in the womb.

Many Christians also think it's up to God how you turn out. You just accept different people for what they are.

Roman Catholics think using embryos for research is wrong. This is because you are a person from the moment of conception.

The Church of Scotland thinks that life is sacred. It should be protected from conception, but the Church agrees with using pre-embryos until the 14th day of development.

Both churches disagree with the idea of designer babies.

ISLAM

Muslims think life is a gift from Allah. He breathes life into the embryo. This is when you become a person. Some Muslims think this happens on the 42nd day of development. Others say it is on the 120th day.

Muslims think that life can be taken in a good cause. So, some agree with embryo research. Some say that Allah has given humans intelligence. We should use this to make life better. If you can make someone's life better by doing embryo research you should.

As long as you do things for the right reasons, Allah will accept what you do. But if you are careless and treat embryos badly for no good reason, then Allah won't be happy.

EGOISM

Egoists wouldn't really worry about embryos being used for research. If the research was good for the Egoist then it would be acceptable.

An Egoist probably wouldn't care where the embryos came from, what was done to them, or what was done with the embryo afterwards. Egoists might think it was fine to buy and sell embryos, as long as this brought benefits. Most other beliefs would probably disagree.

But, if an Egoist thought that using embryos made the world a nastier place, he or she might think again. If we don't mind killing embryos, what might be next?

But if there wasn't any control about using embryos, this could be harmful for the Egoist. An Egoist woman might be forced to give up her eggs (maybe by the Government!) so they could be used for research.

UTILITARIANISM

Utilitarians would think embryo research is acceptable – as long as the good things outweighed the bad ones.

Spare embryos are thrown away anyway, so we might as well use them for something helpful.

Some utilitarians might even think buying and selling embryos was good if it helped people in the end.

Utilitarians think that if embryo research helps people, then the small number of embryos 'killed' is more than balanced by the large numbers of people that are helped.

In war we agree that it is right to kill for good reasons – why not with embryos?

Peter Singer, a Utilitarian, thinks that life ends when your brain dies. So, life must begin when your brain starts working properly. With this argument, you can use embryos till their brains have developed.

This is not really the point for the Utilitarian. If the use of a few helps many people, then that is right.

KEY WORDS

DNA – Chemicals which are like a 'pattern' for making a person. This pattern is called genetic information. It can be changed by scientists and this is called genetic (or gene) therapy (treatment).

Embryo – After the 14th day the cells start to become different parts of the body (differentiation).

Fertilisation/conception – The moment when sperm and egg join. They now collect their information together. This is the pattern for making a person.

Pre-embryo – A collection of cells before the 14th day of development.

Potential person – The idea that everything is there to make you the person you will become in the future, right from the moment of conception.

Quality of life – Life is only worth something once you become a person.

Sacred – Special, holy.

Sanctity of life – Life is sacred and special because it is a gift.

Spare Embryos – Embryos which start to develop but won't be put back into the mother (implanted). They will be destroyed after the 14th day of development.

Sperm/Egg (ovum) – When joined, they form a pre-embryo.

ACTIVITIES

Knowledge & Understanding

1 What do Mr and Mrs Masterton want to do? Do you think they should be allowed?
2 Put the following into the right order.
  a You are now an embryo.
  b The sperm and egg join – conception.
  c At 14 days the cells of the pre-embryo start to form parts of the body.
  d The pre-embryo (blastocyte) develops.
3 People have different ideas about when life begins. Write down two of these ideas.
4 Copy and complete this true/false quiz.
  - DNA is the chemical information which decides what you will be like.
  - You can only use a pre-embryo for tests until it is 7 days old.
  - The HFEA is in charge of embryo research.
  - Believing that life is sacred is the sanctity of life argument.
  - Christians do not believe that life is sacred.
  - An Egoist would always be against embryo research.
  - Spare embryos usually come from IVF treatments.
5 What is so special about the 42nd or 120th day of an embryo's development for a Muslim?

Analysis

1 You think everyone should have the right to choose what kind of child they have (designer babies). Your friend does not think so. In pairs, discuss your views.
2 Some people would like to sell their embryos so that tests could be done on them. From the following list, choose **one** argument supporting the selling of your embryos and **one** against. Which ones do you agree with? Why?
  - It would help scientists make sure they had enough embryos to work on.
  - It could help people who are ill.
  - It could be a way to make money.
  - It is up to the person what they do with their own embryos.
  - No one has the right to sell a human being.
3 If people could choose how their children turned out (designer babies), what would they choose? Ask people in your classroom. What did you find?
4 Peter Singer thinks that life begins when your brain starts working. Do you agree with him? Say what your reasons are.
5 Design a poster to make people think about embryo research. You can either be for it or against it (or in the middle).

Evaluation

'It is always wrong to do research on pre-embryos.' Say whether you agree or not and give **one** reason for your answer.

Assessment question

Outcome 2 (11) Imagine that you are an MSP. You are religious. The Prime Minister wants to make embryo research easier. He's going to get rid of all the rules that scientists have to follow. Write what you would say to him.
Another MSP is an Egoist. Write what he says about your idea.

Homework

Imagine people could sell their embryos. Think of **two** problems that this could cause.

Extension Work

1 Put the words in these sentences into the right order.
  a DNA the for life chemical information is.
  b until You are 14 days old a you're pre-embryo.
  c say life begins Some at conception.
  d means fixing Gene therapy illnesses.
  e gene therapy Some think is God playing.
  f are embryos for used research Spare.
2 Imagine you are a scientist. You do embryo research. Someone sends you a letter. They say horrible things about you. This is because they don't like embryo research. You write back (politely!). What do you say?

LIFE-SUPPORT MACHINES

CASE STUDY

My husband was really fit. He had a good job. He loved his three kids. One morning he juggled boiled eggs for the kids. They thought it was really funny. Then he got in the car. His work was only 15 miles away. An hour later I got a phone call. There had been an accident.

I went to the hospital. He was lying there. There were tubes and machines everywhere.

They said he was 'brain dead'.

But he was warm and breathing. It didn't make sense. The doctor was nice. But he had to ask, 'Did I want to switch off his life-support machine?' They all helped me at the hospital. But they didn't want to get too close. It might be too painful for them.

He'd been juggling boiled eggs just a few hours ago.

KEEPING YOU 'ALIVE'

Most of us only see **life-support machines** on TV shows. Just as well.

Doctors can now keep you 'alive' much longer than in the past.

These machines can pump your blood. They can breathe for you. This makes it difficult for people visiting you because you will be warm, breathing and have a heartbeat. But the doctors will still think you are dead.

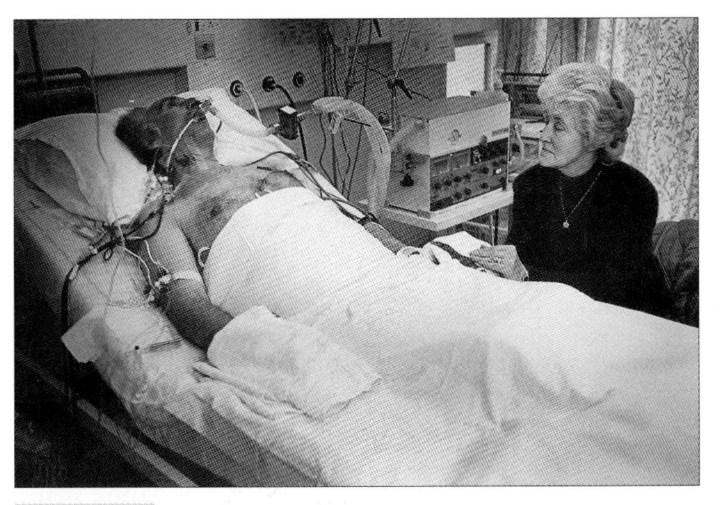

figure 2.4 *Someone on a life-support machine*

Switching off the machines is called **involuntary euthanasia.** Some people think this is just letting you die. Others say that it is helping you die.

Do you think there is a difference between *letting* someone die and *helping* them to die?

When do you die?

Sounds like an easy question. Doctors say you die when you are 'brain stem dead'. This means that your brain is not working any more and you cannot think any more. But you can still be kept breathing and your heart can still be beating. People can also be in what's called a Persistent Vegetative State (**PVS**). What this means is different according to individuals, and doctors aren't always sure how aware the person is about anything. Some people say it's when you're a 'vegetable'. Sometimes, someone in a PVS can be 'kept going' using life-support machines. It is up to your relatives when it is switched off. They might have to try to work out what you would want.

When do you think someone is dead?

Sanctity of life v quality of life

You have already looked at these ideas. Some people use them when they decide whether they should switch off life support.

Sanctity of life

- Life is sacred. We should keep it going for as long as we can.
- Life is sacred, but keeping someone alive on a machine is wrong. We should switch it off and let nature take over.
- Life is sacred, but is someone in a PVS really living?

Quality of life

- How can you have any quality of life wired up to a machine? You should switch it off because a life like that is not worth living.
- But maybe someone in a PVS is having a nice time. We don't know what being in a PVS is like. So it's not up to us to decide to end it.
- People are important to their families too. Maybe we should keep the machines going for them?

Some other concerns

Here are some more problems with this topic:

- What if you switched off the machine and a cure was found for the illness the person had the next day?
- Some people still live a while after the machine has been switched off. How long should we care for them?
- We have to think about what the person who is suffering would want. How can we work that out?
- It is hard for the relatives. They might be pushed into making a quick decision. This might be because doctors want the ill person's organs to transplant. The relatives might disagree about what to do.
- How do relatives know all the facts? Who tells them? They don't want to regret the decision they make.
- Do we know enough about PVS to say that the person is really dead? Doctors don't all agree about how bad a PVS is.

Discussion point

Are you only alive when your brain is working?

Facts and Figures

- There are about 1000–1500 people in a PVS in Britain.
- A poll in 1990 said that 66% of people agree with involuntary euthanasia.
- The longest anyone has been in a PVS is 37 years.

Rights and responsibilities

What rights does a person on life support have? Should you have fewer rights because you're brain dead? Should you only have rights when you're conscious?

What responsibilities do we have for people on life support? What about the people who have a better chance of recovering? Shouldn't we spend our time on them? Is there a 'duty to die'?

Case Study

On 15 April 1989, Tony Bland (17) was crushed in the Hillsborough football disaster. He was in a PVS. His parents wanted to switch off his life support. The case went to court. It even went to the House of Lords. This is the most powerful court in the UK. The House of Lords decided to let his machine be switched off. They said it wasn't doing him any good. His machine was switched off.

MORAL RESPONSES

CHRISTIANITY

Christians have mixed views. Some think that you should use life support to keep a person going as long as you can. Life is sacred so you should always try to save it. Some think you should switch off the machine and let God take over. If you're trying to kill them, that is wrong. But if you are just letting them die naturally that is fine.

Hospices help people who are dying. They don't try to cure people. They think you should just be there for the person till the end.

The Church of Scotland has said that it doesn't agree with ending life on purpose. But, it doesn't see any point in putting death off when it is going to happen anyway.

ISLAM

Muslims think that life should only be ended in a good cause. They think there is no point in keeping someone 'alive' who cannot live a normal life as a complete person.

Some Muslims say it is right to give the dead 'relief' from their agony. This is not killing. It is 'letting die'. This means you hand the dying person over to Allah. It is then up to him what he does.

Muslims say you are dead when your heart and breathing have stopped, and when your brain is not working. Then you can be 'handed over to Allah'. Muslims think it is up to Allah to give and take life.

EGOISM

Egoists also have different views. There is no point in being 'alive' if your life is not worth living. But maybe you should be kept alive at all costs. Maybe they will discover a cure. You can't be cured if you're dead.

If it is someone else, not you – maybe you'd want to 'keep' them. So you would keep the life support going. But, maybe they would be a nuisance and you would switch it off.

Perhaps you would think no one should be kept on life support. It costs money. Your taxes. Maybe you think there are better things to spend it on. But if we just switched off people's life support that might be bad for you – one day. A world like that would not be good for you.

UTILITARIANISM

Utilitarians usually believe in quality of life arguments. Why keep someone on a machine when their life is not worth living any more?

You could also switch off a machine, even if you know that means killing the person. Sometimes killing is the right thing to do when it is good for most people.

Keeping someone on a life-support machine might mean other patients are being ignored. What is the point in wasting your time on someone who is dead anyway? You could be helping someone with a chance instead.

Utilitarians think that life support doesn't always do much good for the person on it. It might also be bad for people in general. So it should be switched off.

KEY WORDS

Euthanasia – Voluntarily ending life with as little pain and suffering as possible.

Involuntary – When you don't choose. Someone does it for you.

Life-support machines – Machines which keep your organs going.

Organs – Parts of your body which make different things work. Many organs can be replaced, like your kidneys, liver, heart, etc.

PVS – When your brain is no longer working normally but your organs can still be kept going.

ACTIVITIES

Knowledge & Understanding

1. What can a life-support machine do?
2. What term is used to explain when your brain is not working any more?
3. Put the following statements under the right heading:

   Sanctity of life argument *Quality of life argument*

   a Life is sacred. We should keep it going as long as we can.

   b Maybe someone in a PVS is having a nice time.

   c Life is sacred, but is someone in a PVS living?

   d How can you have any quality of life when you are wired up to a machine?
4. Why might relatives be 'pushed into a decision'?
5. Copy and complete the sentences using these words:

   Lords good crushed switched PVS off

   On 15 April 1989, Tony Bland (17) was ______ in the Hillsborough disaster. He was in a ____. The House of _______ decided to let his machine be _____________ _____. They said it wasn't doing him any ______.
6. What do hospices do?
7. What does a Muslim mean by saying they hand someone 'over to Allah'?

Analysis

1 You are the woman in the case study on page 21. What do you do about your husband's life-support machine? Write down **two** things you might ask the doctors. Write **two** things you would be thinking about at this time.

2 You are religious. Your brother is an Egoist. Your mum is on a life-support machine. Your brother wants to switch it off, but you don't want to. From the following statements, choose **three** which you think you could use as a religious person to persuade your brother.
   - **a** Life is a gift from God.
   - **b** If life is not worth living we should end it.
   - **c** Mum is taking up the doctor's time. They could be using the machine for someone else.
   - **d** Mum's death could be good for others.
   - **e** We should trust in God to do what is right.
   - **f** We can let people die, but not help them to die.
   - **g** Life is sacred. You should always try to save it.

3 You and your brother still disagree. So a judge has to decide. The judge asks you and your brother questions in court. Act this out in your class.

4 The judge decides your brother is right. Your mum's machine will be switched off. You cannot face talking to your brother. Write him a note explaining how you feel and why you think he is wrong.

5 Design a short information leaflet about life-support machines. This leaflet will be given to relatives of someone on a life-support machine. Use the following points to help you write the leaflet.
   - **a** What is life support?
   - **b** What you might be feeling at this time.
   - **c** Two reasons why you might want to keep the machine switched on.
   - **d** Two reasons why you might want to switch the machine off.

Evaluation

'It is never right to switch off a life-support machine.'
Say whether you agree or not. Give **one** reason for your answer.

Assessment question

Outcome 1 (11) Write a statement from each of the two brothers in Activity 3 above. Each brother should give **one** reason for his beliefs.

Homework

You are a doctor. You are looking after someone on a life-support machine. Her relatives are thinking about switching it off. They ask you this question, 'What would you do, doctor?' What would your answer be?

Extension work

1 Some people make 'living wills'. They write what they would like to happen to them if they ever ended up on a life-support machine. Write your own 'living will'.

2 This is a list of people who might have to make decisions about switching off life-support machines. For each person/group of people, write **one** advantage and **one** disadvantage of making the decision.
   Doctors
   Relatives
   Judges

ORGAN TRANSPLANTS

CASE STUDY

Jetmund Engeset is a surgeon. He is one of Scotland's top surgeons. He thinks that people who die in accidents should have their bodies kept 'alive'. This could be done using life-support machines. We could then use their organs for other people. He doesn't understand why we just bury bodies. He thinks this is a waste because they could be used to help other people. Their organs could be used for transplant.

At the moment you are only kept on life support if it is good for you. This would be keeping people on life support because it is good for others. This would be against the law. Dr Engeset wants the law changed. This would mean people who need organ transplants could get them right away.

Do you think we should keep people 'alive' so that we can use their organs?

figure 2.5 *An organ ready for transplant*

THE NEED FOR TRANSPLANTS

Your body's organs sometimes stop working. This might be after an accident. It might be after an illness. It might be because they wear out. Hearts, lungs, kidneys, and livers can be **transplanted.** This means they are taken from someone else. Sometimes, the person is alive (for example, you can donate one kidney). Sometimes the person has to be dead (only then can you donate your heart).

The person who gets the organ can then lead a more normal life.

Transplants are done all the time. But there are still big questions about how right or wrong they are.

THE RIGHTS OF THE DEAD

When you are alive you have rights. Do you still have them once you are dead? Some people think that once you are a dead body, you aren't 'you' any more. Others disagree. If someone takes your organs when you are dead, have they taken a bit of you? Some think that people should have to donate their organs after they die – even a dead person could have responsibilities!

Some people also think that the organs of babies who die should be used. Some also think that babies who die before they are born should have their organs taken out. The baby might have died because of a **miscarriage.** Or it might have died because of an **abortion.** This is even more difficult: if an adult dies they can say if they want to donate their organs. Babies cannot choose.

What about people in a PVS? Some people think that their organs should be used.

Can you still have responsibilities to others when you are dead?

GIVING

Your organs can only be used when you've filled in a **donor card.** Even then your relatives have to agree. Some people think this is wrong because lots of people just don't bother to get a card (even though they would not mind their organs being used). Some people are a bit superstitious. They think having a donor card might mean they are more likely to die!

This means that there are not enough organs to go round. What could be done about this?

- Some say that everyone should have to donate their organs after death (make it compulsory). This would happen whether you liked it or not – just like paying your taxes!
- Some people say your organs should be used unless you have said that you do not want that. This is called 'opting out'. This already happens in Singapore.

Some people worry that relatives would be pressurised into donating your organs. Doctors might push for it when you are in a PVS. They might also decide you are dead too soon so they can have your organs!

Some organs and body tissues (like bone marrow) can be donated when you are alive. Should you have the right to give away bits of your body? What if you had a child who needed a heart transplant? If you donated your heart you would die. Should you be allowed to? Now, you are not allowed. Maybe if you were, some people might feel you should! It all gets complicated. What about selling your organs?

DISCUSSION POINT

Should people be allowed to sell their organs?

- Some people say this is the same as selling anything else. It is your body. It is your choice. If you are poor, maybe it is the only way to help your family.
- Some say this is wrong because it is the poor being used by the rich. Maybe people would kill others. Then they could sell the victim's organs.

RECEIVING

Who should get organs? At the moment, it is the person who needs them the most. The doctors decide this by judging how ill the person is. Should they think about other things too?

What if there were two people needing a heart transplant? There was only one heart. One of the men was a hard working dad with children. The other was a single man in prison for murder. Which one should get the heart?

Should we spend money on transplants anyway? They are expensive. They don't always work. Should we spend the money on other things in a hospital – things which might do more good?

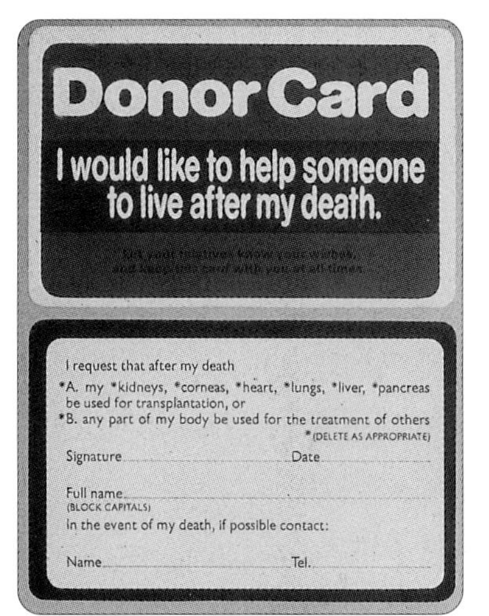

Donor Card

I would like to help someone to live after my death.

I request that after my death
*A. my *kidneys, *corneas, *heart, *lungs, *liver, *pancreas be used for transplantation, or
*B. any part of my body be used for the treatment of others
*(DELETE AS APPROPRIATE)

Signature.................... Date....................

Full name....................
(BLOCK CAPITALS)

In the event of my death, if possible contact:

Name.................... Tel....................

figure 2.6 *A donor card*

What should doctors think about when they are deciding who should get a transplant?

What if someone 'caused' their own illness? What if two people needed a liver transplant? There was only one liver. One person needed it because his liver had been damaged by illness. The other person's liver had been damaged by drinking too much alcohol. Which one should get the liver?

THE APPLIANCE OF SCIENCE

Xenotransplantation

Maybe there would be enough organs if we used animals. The animals could be killed and their organs given to people. This already happens but not often. The person getting the organ needs lots of drugs. This is to make the human body 'accept' the animal's organ. One way to deal

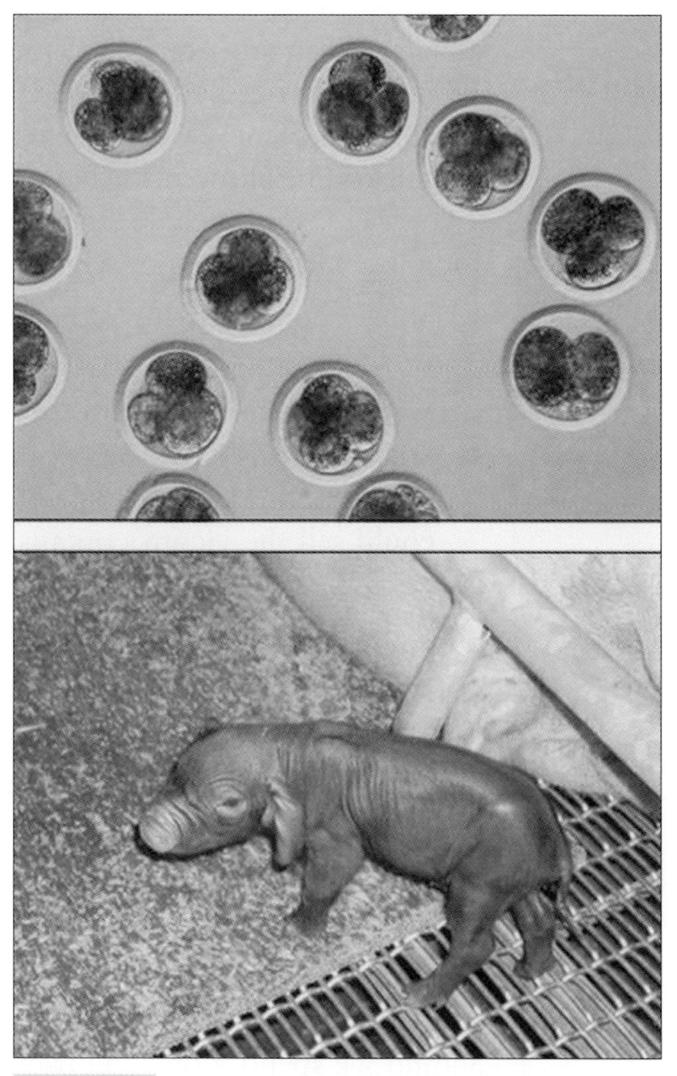

figure 2.7 *Xenotransplantation. This female piglet was cloned by injecting genetic material from fetal pig skin cells into an egg, and transplanting that egg into a surrogate mother*

FACTS AND FIGURES

- There are about 6000 people waiting for transplants in the UK.
- The first ever heart transplant was in 1967.
- Xenotransplantation makes money! It could make about $5 billion over the next 15 years.

with this is to make animal organs more human. You can do this with genetic technology (see page 15).

Some people don't like this because humans might get more animal illnesses. Some people say it is a good idea. It is making use of animals and so is only the same as eating them.

Stem-cell growth/cloning

When a woman has an abortion, cells can be taken from the baby. These can be grown. In the future we might grow organs like this. Cloning means taking one of your own cells and growing organs that way. It will be a while before this can be done with humans.

Bionics

Maybe we could replace human organs with *machines*. We would then be part-robot!

MORAL RESPONSES

CHRISTIANITY

Some **Christians** agree with transplants. They think your body should stay 'whole'. If you want to donate your organs you can, but it should not be compulsory. Then it would not be you choosing to do something good. Christians do not think you should be able to sell your organs. This would be the rich taking advantage of the poor.

The Roman Catholic Church thinks using things from aborted babies is wrong. The Church of Scotland isn't sure. Most Christians don't mind using animals for organs. But the animals must not suffer. Christians believe that donating your organs shows you follow the teaching 'Love your neighbour'.

ISLAM

Muslims have different views. Some think that transplants are wrong. On judgement day your body has to be brought back to life. There should not be anything missing.

Some Muslims think you should donate your organs. This is showing kindness to others.

Muslims do not agree with selling organs. This is taking advantage of the poor. You should help the poor in other ways.

Muslims would not agree with using some animals for organs. Muslims think pigs are 'unclean' (haram). So you could not use a pig organ to replace your own.

Muslims think that being able to transplant organs gives people power. You should use this power well.

EGOISM

An **Egoist** would not donate give his organs unless he got something back for them. Egoists might think selling your organs was fine if it made you money. An Egoist who needed an organ would like to be able to buy one.

Egoists would not really mind where organs came from. Aborted babies, people in a PVS, animals. All of these would be fine if they could help the Egoist.

Egoists would also be happy to support scientists who were trying to find better ways to get hold of organs.

An Egoist might not like compulsory organ donation. He might also worry that a doctor could decide he was dead too quickly, so that the doctor could use the Egoist's organs.

UTILITARIANISM

Utilitarians say that donating organs is fine if the good things outweigh the bad ones.

If things are properly controlled then organ donation should not be a problem. Even selling organs might be good if the sellers were protected.

Utilitarians would probably think that it was a good idea to use people's organs unless they said 'no' up front (opting out). This would produce a lot of happiness and not 'cost' anything.

Some Utilitarians would say that hanging on to your organs after you are dead does not make any sense. They are no use to you then. But they might be of use to someone else!

Utilitarians would not worry where organs came from as long as this did not cause any suffering. You could take organs from aborted babies (who are being killed anyway). You could take organs from people in a PVS because maybe they would never come out of the PVS anyway. You can use animals as long as they don't suffer. Some Utilitarians might be worried about using animals. This is because it could mean humans getting more diseases.

Utilitarians would want to make sure that the bad things about organ transplants were outweighed by the good things.

KEY WORDS

Abortion – When a woman decides to end her pregnancy.

Donor Card – A card which you carry with you. It says that if you die, doctors can take your organs for other people.

Miscarriage – When a woman's baby dies in the womb.

Transplant – Taking an organ from one body and putting it in another.

Xenotransplantation – Using animal organs to replace human ones.

ACTIVITIES

Knowledge & Understanding

1 Why does Jetmund Engeset want to keep dead bodies 'alive'?
2 Write down **one** reason why you might need a transplant.
3 Where can organs come from?
4 Copy and complete:
Some people say that you should have to donate your organs. It should be ______. Other people think your organs should be used unless you have said you don't want that. This is called '______'. Some people worry that ______ might be ______ into donating your organs.

Words: **pressurised**, **relatives**, **opting out**, **compulsory**.
5 Write down **one** reason why some people think selling body organs is wrong.
6 From this list of statements about organ transplants, copy **two** which a Utilitarian might agree with. Write **one** reason why you have chosen each one.
  a You should not use pigs for transplants.
  b The body should stay whole for judgement day.
  c Using things from aborted babies is wrong.
  d Who cares where organs come from.
  e You should be able to buy an organ when you need it.
  f Getting organs should not involve any suffering.
  g Selling organs might be alright if sellers are protected.
  h Using animals might mean people get animal diseases.

Analysis

1 You are at a meeting with Dr Engeset. You get the chance to ask him a question. What question would you ask?
2 You are the person who wants to give his heart to his child. Write a short letter to the doctor explaining why you want to do this.
3 The government decides to let people sell their organs. Think of **three** rules there should be about this.
4 A laboratory is to be built in your town. Here, animals will be used to grow organs for human transplant. There is a public meeting about it. The following things are said. Find **one** example of something which a Muslim, Christian, Egoist and Utilitarian would say.
  a I hope the animals won't suffer.
  b Pig organs should not be used for people.
  c This will give us lots of power. I hope it is used well.
  d I hope this will help me. I don't care about the animals.
  e Could this mean people getting animal diseases?
  f Will the good things about this outweigh the bad ones?
  g Will this all be properly controlled?

Evaluation

'Religious people should *have* to donate their organs.' Write **one** argument for this statement and **one** against. Also write your own view about it.

Assessment question

Outcome 3 (11) 'People should be allowed to sell their organs.'
Copy and complete:
I think this statement is right/wrong. I think this for two reasons.
First of all, I think.. .
I also think... .

Homework

Find out how many people in your family have a donor card. Choose one person and ask them why they do or don't have a donor card.

Extension work

1 Design a poster which makes people think about carrying a donor card.
2 You are the wife of the 'hard-working dad' on page 29. The doctors decide the murderer needs the heart more than your husband. What might you say to the doctors?
3 Find out which body organs can already be replaced by machines.

VOLUNTARY EUTHANASIA

CASE STUDY

Derek Humphry's wife had cancer. In 1975 he helped her to kill herself. They both thought it is up to you when you die. Derek set up groups who believed the same as him. By 1990 he was in charge of the World Federation of Right to Die Societies.

Derek says that they are not killers. They don't just want to get rid of people. They don't want to help them run away from their problems. The Federation cares about people. They share their problems. They don't think people should have to suffer. He argues that we need laws to give people more choice.

In 1980 the Voluntary Euthanasia Society of Scotland published a book. It was called, *How to Die with Dignity*. It was written by a doctor. It described the best ways to take your own life.

figure 2.8 *Derek Humphry*

WHY DIE?

Voluntary euthanasia means you decide when, where and how you die. Why would you do this?

- If you were ill and in lots of pain you might want it to end quickly.
- Maybe you didn't like your life any more. If you lost something important like your sight, you might not want to live.
- Maybe you just want to make your own choices about death.
- Maybe you don't want to be a **burden** to others.

There are two kinds of euthanasia:

- **Active:** You take your life on purpose. You might take an overdose of drugs.
- **Passive:** You don't let doctors save your life.

In Britain, voluntary euthanasia is not against the law. But it is against the law to help someone die. This is sometimes called **assisted suicide**. You could be charged with murder.

Some people think doctors should be able to help you. This is because they know what they are doing. They can make death painless. But even a doctor could be charged with murder if they helped you die. Is that right?

DISCUSSION POINT

What would be good and bad about letting doctors help you end your life?

figure 2.9 *Diane Pretty, who has motor neurone disease, is appealing for the right to die*

The right to die?

Discussion point

Can you do anything you want with your life?

People who agree with voluntary euthanasia say that it is up to you when and how you die. It is your choice. Just like everything else in life.

Other people disagree. They say our life does not just belong to us. Also, if voluntary euthanasia was **legal** people might take advantage of you.

Supporting voluntary euthanasia

Here are some reasons why people think voluntary euthanasia is good.

- It gives you control over your life.
- It is sometimes the kindest thing. It can put you out of your misery.
- It could make life easier for your relatives. They would not have to look after you for ages. It means doctors don't have to spend lots of time with you. They could be helping people who might get better.
- Doctors are there to help you. They have the medical knowledge to help you die painlessly. But they're not allowed to do this.
- What is the point in suffering when you don't have to? Life is only good when you are not in pain. Voluntary euthanasia can stop the pain.
- It would make the world a kinder place. You would not have to worry about getting ill and being in terrible pain. You would know you could end it.

Against voluntary euthanasia

Some people do not think voluntary euthanasia is a good idea. Here are the reasons why.

- Nobody is completely free. You are not allowed to kill someone else. Why should you be allowed to kill yourself? If you were free to kill yourself you might be pressurised into it.
- Voluntary euthanasia is running away from things. When you are dying you might have to 'face up' to your

life. So might your family. If you just end it you are not facing up to things. Your family should help you right to the end. Not help you hurry up the end. Also, your family should not think of you as a nuisance.

- Sometimes suffering can bring good things.
- People are not scared of death. They are scared of dying. They don't need to be. Doctors can make sure you don't have much pain at the end. Also, voluntary euthanasia might put too much pressure on the doctor.
- Life is always worth living. You cannot put a value on life. If you say some lives are worthier of living than others, that is wrong. If we let people end their lives because they are in pain what next? Maybe they should be allowed to die because they are not very happy.
- There are no good reasons for making voluntary euthanasia easy. It would put too much pressure on too many people. Maybe you would end your life before you wanted to. Maybe you would not want to put your family to 'any trouble'. It could make everybody a bit nervous. Maybe someone might say you should get voluntary euthanasia. Maybe even when you don't really want it.

figure 2.10 *Caring for the dying*

Case Study

Dr Jack Kervorkian is in jail. He thinks everyone should be allowed to kill themselves if they want to. He invented a machine to help people do this. The person just pushes a button. This injects drugs into their body. These drugs kill you. Dr Kervorkian made a video. It showed him helping someone to die. A judge said that was enough for a conviction. His lawyers are trying to get him out of jail.

In Holland, doctors can help people to die. There are very strict rules about this. The person must be over 16. This was decided by the Dutch government on 28 December 2000. Some people think it is wrong.

Facts and Figures

- They tried to ban Derek Humphry's book, *Final Exit*. The ban did not work.
- In the USA, 11 doctors have been charged with murder or manslaughter. This is because they helped people to die.
- The British Medical Association disagrees with voluntary euthanasia.

Some 'final' questions

- At what age should you be allowed to take your own life?
- How would people know it was your own decision?
- Who should decide about voluntary euthanasia? Doctors? The government? Judges?

Moral responses

Christianity

Most **Christians** think voluntary euthanasia is wrong. Only God should take life away. In 1981, the Church of Scotland said: 'God is in charge of life'. So you should never kill a person – even if they ask you to. In 1997, the Church of Scotland wrote a document saying what it thinks about the topic:

- Human life does not belong to us. It is God's.
- We are made to be like God. So we have special responsibilities.
- Jesus suffered. Suffering is part of being human.
- We are all responsible for each other. Letting euthanasia happen is wrong.

The Church thinks that we should not need euthanasia. We should care for the dying instead.

The Roman Catholic Church thinks that euthanasia is 'hopeless'. God gives us the job of caring for the dying. In 1991 the Pope said that euthanasia goes against God's law.

ISLAM

Muslims think that only Allah can take away life. You should face up to what Allah sends you. Even if this means suffering.

You must accept your death. This is because it is Allah's will. It shows you follow him (see Surah 31:17).

You should not ask your doctor to help you end your life. You are making him a murderer. He would go to hell then (see Surah 4:93).

When you are dying this is seen as a chance. It is a chance for other Muslims to help you.

EGOISM

Egoists believe you are totally free to do what you want. If you want to take your own life, that is up to you. It doesn't matter why you want to end your life. It is your business.

Egoists would want euthanasia to be easy to do. They would not want to suffer. They would not worry about what the doctor might feel.

Egoists would not really worry about euthanasia being abused. Unless it was the Egoist who was being abused.

UTILITARIANISM

Utilitarians think that life's good things should outweigh the bad ones. If you were suffering then you should be able to end it.

As long as your choice was a free one it is up to you.

Utilitarians might say that voluntary euthanasia can make society 'happier'. This is because you would never have to worry about dying slowly and painfully. You could always ask a doctor to help. Even if that meant killing you.

Some Utilitarians say that doctors already do this sometimes. So you should make it legal.

If society wants people to be happy, it won't ban euthanasia. People should have choices.

However, Utilitarians would want to make sure that euthanasia did not get abused.

KEY WORDS

Active – Doing something on purpose.

Assisted suicide – When someone (usually a doctor) helps you carry out voluntary euthanasia.

Burden – When you feel you are a pest for someone.

Dying with dignity – A term used by supporters of euthanasia to express their belief that dying your own way, when you want is a matter of personal choice.

Legal – When the law lets something happen.

Passive – Letting something happen.

Voluntary – Making a decision for yourself.

ACTIVITIES

Knowledge & Understanding

1 What did Derek Humphry do? Why did he do it?

2 Give **one** situation when someone might want to die.

3 From this list of arguments choose **one** which supports euthanasia and **one** which is against it.
- You should be free to do it if you want.
- Sometimes suffering can bring good things.
- People are not scared of death. They are scared of dying. They don't need to be. Doctors can make sure you don't have much pain at the end.
- It is sometimes the kindest thing. It can put you out of your misery.

4 Why is Dr Jack Kervorkian in prison?

5 At what age do you think you should be able to end your life?

6 What does the Pope think about voluntary euthanasia?

7 Copy and complete:
An Egoist would support/oppose* voluntary euthanasia. This is because

____

____

____

_______________.

* Choose one.

Analysis

1 Do this questionnaire in your class.

a Do you think people should be allowed to choose when to end their lives?
Yes ☐ No ☐ Don't Know ☐
Comments _______________
____

b Should doctors be able to offer euthanasia?
Yes ☐ No ☐ Don't Know ☐
Comments _______________
____

c If voluntary euthanasia was made legal in Scotland, do you think people would abuse it?
Yes ☐ No ☐ Don't Know ☐
Comments _______________
____

d Would you think about voluntary euthanasia if you were dying?
Yes ☐ No ☐ Don't Know ☐
Comments _______________
____

Write a summary of what you find out. You should share this with your class.

2 Design a poster for or against voluntary euthanasia. Display this in your class.

3 Here are some cases where a doctor has helped people to die. Working in pairs, one of you should think up **one** reason why in this case the doctor was right. The other should think of **one** reason why the doctor was wrong.

Nadim was 18. He was a really good football player. He wanted to be a professional. He had a car accident. He ended up in a wheelchair. He would never walk again. That was the end of his football dreams.

Alison was 33. She had an illness called Alzheimer's. You forget things. You can't do things for yourself. She didn't want her two children to see her like that.

Alan was 67. He had cancer. He only had a few months to live. His wife had died of the same thing.

Marion was 48. She was single. She'd had some bad relationships. She was depressed. She said she was going to kill herself anyway.

Evaluation

Helping someone to die is against the law. Do you think the law should be changed so it is not against the law?

Give **one** reason for your answer.

Assessment question

Outcome 3 (11) 'It is up to you when you end your life' Do you agree? Give **two** reasons for your answer.

Homework

You are a judge in the case of Marion. You have to decide what should happen to the doctor who helped her die. Write what you think should happen. Give **two** reasons for your decision.

Extension work

1 Imagine the government made voluntary euthanasia legal. What rules should there be about it? Make a list of **five** rules you think there should be.

2 Here is an outline for a newspaper article about voluntary euthanasia. Complete the blank sections.

What is the fuss about voluntary euthanasia?

by [your name]

In the old days people just died. Sometimes it was painful. Sometimes it took a long time. Nowadays people want to ask their doctors to help. But not to cure them . . . to help them die!

Why might someone want voluntary euthanasia?

[list one or two reasons here].

____

______________________________.

But many people are against it, they say:

[list one or two reasons here].

____

______________________________.

Religious people are leading the campaign against voluntary euthanasia. Rev Jock McFie of the Church of Scotland says:

[write here what a Church of Scotland Minister might say against voluntary euthanasia]

____

______________________________.

But Alan Pieman, a Utilitarian, doesn't agree, he says:

[write here what a Utilitarian might say against Rev McFie]

____

______________________________.

Who knows what to think? There's definitely lots of discussion. What do I think? You maybe don't care, but here goes anyway:

[write here your views about voluntary euthanasia].

____

______________________________.

[suitable drawing or photo here]

3 HUMAN RELATIONSHIPS

SEXUAL BEHAVIOUR

IT'S ONLY NATURAL

DISCUSSION POINT

Should there be 'rules' about sex?

There have always been 'rules' about sex. Who you can have it with, at what age you can have it. In some places you could be punished for having the wrong kind of sex. Some people think there should still be rules. Others think sex is just natural and there should not be rules.

CASE STUDY

A sample of 129 fourteen and fifteen year olds in Ayrshire were asked: 'Why do you think younger people are having sex?' 41% of girls said: 'to impress or look cool' compared with 19% of the boys. 21% of girls said they felt they had to have sex to keep or please their partners.

Scotland on Sunday, 20 August 2000 (adapted)

CASE STUDY

Nurses want to give pupils morning-after pills

School nurses want to be able to give out morning-after emergency contraceptive pills to any pupil who wants them in Scottish secondary schools.

Sunday Herald, 27 August 2000 (adapted)

YOU CAN'T AVOID SEX

Everywhere you turn nowadays you see sex. Younger and younger children can see things in magazines and on TV that their parents couldn't when they were young.

Pornography

A large percentage of people have the internet. This makes it easy to get hold of very strong **pornographic** material. There are far more TV stations now, showing more pornographic images. Some think that laws about pornography are not as strict as they used to be.

Sexier exposure

Is sex more obvious these days? So what?

Teenage – and pre-teen – magazines talk about sex openly. Pop videos are often very sexual. Many popular teenage stars use **sex appeal** to make them more popular. Stars like Britney Spears and programmes like *Buffy the Vampire Slayer* are helped by their sexy image. More TV adverts use sexy images. There has also been an increase in the sales of 'lad mags' like *FHM*. Some people think these are soft pornography.

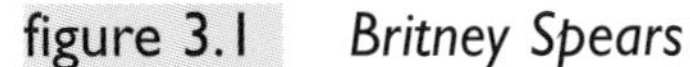

figure 3.1 *Britney Spears*

figure 3.2 *Even companies like Marks and Spencer use sex to sell*

THE AGE OF CONSENT

In Scotland a man and woman can have sex when they are 16 or over. At 16, the law thinks you are grown up enough to cope with sex. Some people are physically ready for sex at a younger age. Some people think that the age of consent should be lower because:

- You should be able to do it when you are ready.
- People will do it when they want anyway.
- It would stop sex being seen as 'dirty' if it was out in the open.

Some disagree. They think the **age of consent** should stay the same – or even be higher, because:

- You might not be mentally ready at 16.
- Making it lower could make people feel pressure to have sex before they are ready.
- You cannot change a law because people are breaking it anyway.
- Lowering the age might mean more people abuse young children.

What should the age of consent be?

- Sex is complicated. It is too much to handle when you're under 16.
- There would be too much **casual sex** if the age of consent was lower.

SAME-SEX RELATIONSHIPS

CASE STUDY

In 1999/2000 there was a lot of disagreement about the 'Section 2A' issue. This part of the law says that teachers shouldn't say that homosexuality is a good way of life. If a teacher said it was 'OK to be gay' they would be breaking the law. The Scottish Parliament wanted to change this. Brian Souter, the boss of the Stagecoach bus company, wanted section 2A to stay. He organised a referendum. 66% of Scots did not vote. But 89% of those who did vote, supported Mr Souter's view. However, the Scottish Parliament did get rid of Section 2A in the end.

Homosexuality means loving and sometimes having sex with people of the same sex. There have probably always been homosexuals. It was against the law to be homosexual in the UK until recently.

Being thought of as 'gay' is sometimes a big fear for teenagers. But most schools must have some people who are. Some people believe that you go through phases when you're a teenager. You might think you are gay for a while but might turn out not to be. You should be helped through these times. Eventually you'll end up in a 'normal' relationship.

Others say that if you end up gay there is nothing wrong with that. Here are some views on homosexuality:

- Being gay is up to you.
- As long as both people involved are grown up, it is no one else's business.
- You are born gay – you can't change it.
- Being gay is no worse than being straight.

But there are views that say:

- Being gay is not natural.

- It is like being sick and you need to be cured.
- Gay people are more casual about sex. This can cause problems.

Gay people think anti-gay beliefs are **prejudiced.** Others think that young people should be protected from gay relationships.

Is it wrong to be gay?

figure 3.3 *This gay couple used a surrogate mother to produce their twin babies*

- 32% of 15 year old boys and 37% of 15 year old girls say they have had sex.
- In 1999 a male gay couple used surrogate mothers to produce their own family.
- If a girl first has sex at 12 she has much more chance of catching a sexually-transmitted disease than an older girl.

LOVE OR LUST?

Is sex special? Some people think it is only for pleasure. As long as it is two adults and no one gets hurt then what's the problem? It is just the same as doing anything else together.

Other people don't think this. They say that sex is very special. Sex means something between two people. You should be **committed** to that person.

You can show this commitment by getting married. Once you are married you should only have sex with your husband/wife. Even if you only live with someone you should be faithful to them. Some people think casual sex is wrong because it can lead to more problems between people.

Should you be committed to someone before you have sex with them?

Moral responses

Christianity

Christians believe that sex is a gift from God. It should only happen in marriage. In 1994, the Church of Scotland said that Sex is a blessing from God. You don't need to be ashamed of it. It should only take place when you are married.

Casual sex is wrong because it means you are not showing your commitment to the other person. The age of consent should not be too low. If it was, this could mean that adults will abuse children. You also need to be grown up enough to cope with sex.

In 1967 the Church of Scotland said that being gay was; 'a weakness'. In 1994 it said that it still thinks that being gay is not what God wants.

The Roman Catholic Church teaches that practising homosexuality is wrong, although it tries to show care for people who are gay.

Both Churches think that gay people should not be badly treated though.

Christian texts about sex: Leviticus 18:22; Genesis 19:1–11; Judges 19:16–30; Romans 1:24–27; 1 Corinthians 6:9–11.

Islam

Muslims also think that sex should only happen when married. You can be married to more than one person though (if you are a man).

The Qur'an has strict rules about sex, and severe punishments. You can be stoned to death for having sex with someone when you are married to someone else (Surahs 4:15–16 and 24:2).

There are different views about the age of consent. But people should always be protected from abuse whatever age they are.

Being gay is totally against Muslim teaching. Muslims think it is not natural. They believe that Allah is unhappy about anyone being gay.

Gay sex can be punished because the partners are unmarried. Being the same sex, they could not be married legally in Britain.

EGOISM

Egoists would think that whether you have sex is up to you. You are a free person – so you should be able to have sex how, when and with who you want to.

The age of consent should be when you personally feel ready for sex. Some Egoists might say that there should be no laws about sex if having sex doesn't harm you.

Being gay is also up to you. If you enjoy gay sex, then no one should stop you having it.

The Egoist might say that sex is the most natural thing there is. If you want to do it, watch it, read about it then that is your choice. There should be no silly rules about it.

The only rules an Egoist might want would be rules to protect him. For example, maybe much more casual sex would mean more sexually transmitted diseases. This could harm the Egoist. The Egoist would also want rules to protect him or her from being raped.

UTILITARIANISM

Utilitarians would think you are free to do what you want – as long as this does not harm anyone else.

Too much casual sex might cause social problems. This would not be good.

Homosexuality is acceptable if it doesn't make society unbalanced (perhaps by fewer children being born).

The age of consent should be set to balance out pleasure and protect young people.

KEY WORDS

Age of consent – The age when sex is legal.

Casual sex – Having sex without commitment.

Commitment – Being 'tied' to one person by your own choice.

Homosexuality – Same-sex relationships.

Pornography – Images showing sexual activity and/or naked bodies.

Prejudice – Making a decision about something before you know the full facts. Pre-judging someone.

Sex appeal – Sexual attractiveness.

ACTIVITIES

Knowledge & Understanding

1 What kind of 'rules' are there about sex?
2 What did 41% of girls say the reason was for people having sex at a younger age?
3 What **one** thing might make it easier to see pornography these days?
4 Some people think the age of consent should be lower than 16. Give **one** reason why they think so.
5 Why do some people think it is wrong to be gay?
6 Copy and complete:
In 1994, the Church of ________ said:
'Sex is a ________ from God. You don't need to be ________ of it. It should only take place when you are ________.'
Words: **ashamed, married, blessing, Scotland.**
7 Copy and complete, choosing the right options from the choices in *italics*:
Being gay is totally *against/supported by* Muslim teaching. Muslims think it is *natural/not natural.* They believe that Allah is *happy/unhappy* about *men/anyone* being gay.

Analysis

1 Write your own answer to these two problem page letters:
  a *I am 14 years old. My boyfriend is 17. He wants me to have sex with him. He says if I love him I would. What should I do?*
  b *I am a 16 year-old boy at Secondary school. I fancy this guy in my class. I think he likes me too. What should I do?*
2 Find **three** examples of 'soft pornography' from newspapers. Write a sentence under each explaining why someone might think it is wrong.
3 Discuss in groups: 'The age of consent in Scotland should be 14'. Write down two points of view which are shared by more than one person.
4 Neil is a religious person. He is 20. He wants to have sex with his girlfriend. His friend, David, who is also religious, thinks this is wrong. Act out their discussion as a short role play.

Evaluation

'Sex should only happen when you are in a long-term relationship.'
Do you agree? Give **two** reasons for your answer.

Assessment question

Outcome 2 The age of consent has been lowered to 12 years old. This has made people who disagree with it go to people's doors to ask them if they agree with this change in the law. What would an Egoist and a religious person say?

Homework

Carry out a survey asking the question: 'At what age should it be legal to have sex?'

Extension work

1 Complete the following table, putting the statements below into the right column.
- Who you have sex with is up to you.
- Sex is a blessing from God.
- Sex should only happen between two people who are married.
- You need to be grown up to cope with sex.
- You can be stoned to death for having sex with someone else while you are married.
- If you enjoy gay sex then no one should stop you having it.
- The Roman Catholic Church teaches that being gay is wrong.

Moral stance	*Belief*
Christian	
Muslim	
Egoist	
Utilitarian	

2 Write some more problem page letters. Pass them to your friends to answer.
3 Watch a pop video (for example, *Baby one more time* by Britney Spears) Write **two** things in the video which could be examples of 'sex appeal'.

MARRIAGE AND ITS ALTERNATIVES

Anne is 24. John is 28. They have just got married. Are they normal? Anne says:

CASE STUDY

We met at work and we really liked each other. We'd just sit and ignore everyone else! We went out together. We found that we were the same kind of people. People at work started to ask us if we'd 'done it yet'! After ten months we decided to get married. We did this a year later. We never had sex before getting married. We had a church wedding but we're not really religious. We're going to have children soon. Then I'll give up work. John gets paid better than me. We're glad we got married and didn't just live together. Getting married shows you really care about each other.

WHAT IS MARRIAGE FOR?

Marriage is not just about two people. Some people think it keeps society together. Some people think it is just silly and old-fashioned.

People who think marriage is a good thing say:

- It is very public. You make promises in front of many people. This means you have to stick to them. If you are religious you have made promises to God too.
- It is a legal agreement. So, you will have to try to make it work out.
- It joins both families. They can help out if things get tough.
- It makes it easier to bring up children. They are hard work after all!
- It keeps sex under control!

Some people think it is better to have an 'open marriage'. This means you are married to one person but can have sex with others. Some disagree, they say that the point of marriage is you only have sex with one person.

Do you think an 'open marriage' is a good idea?

Just a piece of paper?

Some say that living together (**co-habitation**) has all the good points of marriage anyway. You can still show how much you care about each other if you live together. You can still have the same rights – and so can your children.

Some say this isn't true. They think that people who just live together are more likely to fall out. Sometimes living together is just trying things out. This makes it a 'second best' kind of relationship. But people who like the idea of living together think it is better. Sometimes married people stick it out in a miserable relationship because it is so difficult to get out of. That can't be good.

Discussion Point

Do you think it's better to live together or get married?

Just one person – boring?

In most places in the world you are married to just one person at a time. This is called **monogamy**. In some places you can have more than one partner at a time. This is called **polygamy**. Some male Muslims and a few male Christians do this. They say it is one good way of looking after women. There are lots of arguments against it too.

What do you think of polygamy?

figure 3.4 *A church wedding*

PLAYING THE FIELD

Some think that any kind of long-term relationship is a bad idea. It is best to be free. You can have relationships with as many people as you want for as long as you want. You could have a whole string of 'one-night stands'. Supporters say this keeps everyone happy. So society will be happy too. Better than a long-term relationship which has gone off. Others disagree. They say that this kind of freedom is too risky. There is too much chance of getting hurt. There is no emotional security.

DISCUSSION POINT

Are gay marriages just the same as straight marriages? Should gay couples be allowed to have children?

GAY MARRIAGE

In Holland, gay marriages are legal. Gay people say they should be allowed to marry too. They want to show the world they love each other just like straight couples do. They can even have children, by using IVF and donated eggs or sperm (see page 14). People who disagree say that marriage should only be for men and women.

figure 3.5 *Gay marriage*

FACTS AND FIGURES

- In 1990 about 25% of births in Scotland were to unmarried women.
- About 50–70% of men will have an affair once married. A survey said that 70% of people thought being 'faithful' was the most important thing in a marriage.
- In 1990, 55% of Scots were married. There were 34,600 new marriages that year.

ARRANGED MARRIAGE

This is normal in many places in the world. It means your partner is chosen for you. Some people don't like it because:

- If someone is chosen for you, you didn't fall in love with them yourself.
- You should be free to choose who you want to marry.
- Marriage is between you and your partner. Your family just have to put up with it.

Many people think arranged marriages are good. Here's why:

- Love can grow. Falling in love with someone isn't always the best way to start a relationship.
- Parents have more experience. They can make better choices than you. Anyway, you can always say no.
- Marriages are also between families. If they all get on at the start this is better. This makes society better.

DISCUSSION POINT

What do you think might be good and bad about having your marriage arranged?

THE FUTURE

Will marriage die out? Or will it get trendy again? Some think it will survive. This is because life is getting more complicated. Being married is the best way for a couple to cope with this.

Do you think marriage is out of date?

MORAL RESPONSES

CHRISTIANITY

Christians think that marriage is best. In 1992, the Church of Scotland said:

- *God wants people to be in long-term relationships.*
- *Men and women should be together. That is God's way.*
- *Marriage helps control sex.*
- *Jesus went to a wedding, (John 2) so he must think marriage is right.*
- *The Apostle Paul thinks marriage is right (e.g. 1 Corinthians 7).*

Some Christians say that Genesis 2:24 explains why marriage is best. It is an agreement watched over by God.

Some Christians think living together first is all right. Others don't think this shows enough care for each other. Most Christians don't agree with polygamy.

Most Christians do not like the idea of gay marriage. They also don't think much of arranged marriage. But in the Salvation Army you can only marry another Salvation Army member if you are an officer.

Roman Catholics think of marriage as holy. It is everlasting.

A man will leave his father and mother and become one with his wife. They are now one. Man shouldn't split what God has put together.

Mark 10:6–9

ISLAM

Muslims also think marriage is important. It protects women. It helps keep children secure. (See Surahs 4:25; 7:189.)

Muslims agree with arranged marriages. They think 'love marriages' don't always work. But Muslims can reject their parents' choice of partner if they want (Surah 4:3).

Muhammed had ten wives! Some Muslims still believe in polygamy. They think this is a way to care for women without a husband. But you have to be able to treat all your wives in the same way (Surah 4:129). Some Muslims think this is impossible. So they only have one wife at a time.

Muslims don't really like the idea of living together. They also think gay marriages are wrong, because it is wrong to be gay.

EGOISM

Egoists will support marriage if it suits them, and not if it doesn't.

It is good if marriage protects you or keeps your relationship strong. But it is bad if it ties you down.

You might like an arranged marriage because it saves you going to the trouble of finding someone! You might also hate it because you didn't get to choose your partner. If you are an Egoist parent, you might like controlling your child's future in this way.

If you are gay and you want to marry your partner, that is up to you. Any rules about marriage are only good if they make your life better.

UTILITARIANISM

Utilitarians think marriage is good if it keeps society right. But if living together gave you the same rights as a married couple, then that would be just as good. Marriage should look after the rights of the man and the woman.

If arranged marriages work, then there is nothing wrong with them. But if they put pressure on the couple then they won't lead to happiness.

Gay marriages are fine, as long as they don't mean fewer children being born. This might unbalance society. Any kind of relationship is fine if most people benefit from it.

KEY WORDS

Arranged marriage – Where your partner is chosen for you (usually by your parents).

Co-habitation – Living together without being married.

Marriage – Where two people are joined together as a couple. Usually with a legal contract.

Monogamy – Having one wife or husband at a time.

Polygamy – Having more than one wife or husband at a time.

ACTIVITIES

Knowledge & Understanding

1 Do you think that not having sex before you are married is old-fashioned?

2 In your own words, give one reason why marriage might still be a good idea today.

3 Do you think living together is 'second best'? Give a reason for your answer.

4 Match the following words with their explanations:
Words: marriage, co-habitation, monogamy, polygamy, arranged marriage.
- Having one wife or husband at a time.
- Having more than one wife or husband at a time.
- Living together without being married.
- Where two people are joined together as a couple. Usually with a legal contract.
- Where your partner is chosen for you (usually by your parents).

5 Write **one** good reason for having an arranged marriage.

6 What do you think a Christian would think of living together and not getting married?

7 From the three moral stances of Religious authority (Christianity/Islam), Egoism and Utilitarianism, which ones might say the following?
  a Marriage is best.
  b Marriage is holy.
  c Having more than one wife at a time is not wrong.
  d There is no problem with gay marriage.
  e There are good things about arranged marriages.
  f There are bad things about arranged marriages.

Analysis

1 Act out a role play as follows:
You and your partner are 19 years old. You want to live together. Your mum is very religious and she thinks this is wrong. How do you convince her . . . nicely!

2 Make a short information leaflet that tries to persuade people to get married and not live together. Use the following information as headings and write your own explanation of them.
- Marriage shows you really care
- Being married means you will try harder to make the relationship work
- It is better for your children if you are married
- Marriage doesn't need to make you feel 'tied down'
- Marriage keeps both families happy
- Marriage is better for society

Evaluation

'Marriage is much better than just living together.' Do you agree? Give **two** reasons for your answer.

Assessment question

Outcome 2 (11) What would an Egoist and a religious person think about arranged marriage?

Homework

Ask a married couple you know to tell you why they got married instead of living together.
or
Ask a co-habiting couple why they choose not to get married. Make sure they don't mind you using their reasons in the class.

Extension work

1 You want to arrange your child's marriage. He/she doesn't think much of the idea. Write them a short note explaining why you think this is a good idea.

2 Copy and complete this poster idea:

DIVORCE

CASE STUDY

A study has said that parents need to learn how to help their children through divorce. Some children blame themselves. One said, 'If I'd kept my room tidy my dad wouldn't have left home.' About two out of five marriages in Scotland end in divorce. Children don't seem to be told much about it all by their parents. One boy said his dad said he was 'going away for a while". He never came back. Most children said that all they wanted was to know their parents still loved them.

Sunday Herald, 27 August 2000 (adapted)

CAUSES OF DIVORCE

There are more **divorces** nowadays. Maybe this is because life is harder. Maybe it is because people don't care so much about marriage. In Scotland you can get a divorce if the court/judge thinks the marriage has completely ended (**irretrievable breakdown**).

What kinds of things might cause divorce?

- Having an affair with someone else (**infidelity/adultery**).
- Growing apart. You might change and become 'different people' as you get older.
- Pressures of work/adult life. This might put stress on your relationship.

In Scotland you can get a divorce for:

- Behaving badly towards each other (unreasonable behaviour).
- Adultery.
- Leaving your partner for at least two years (**desertion**).
- Being apart for two years, where both of you agree to be apart (**separation**).
- Being apart for five years where one of you does not agree to be apart.

DISCUSSION POINT

What do you think are the main reasons for divorce?

Most people think that being married has its good times and bad times. Sometimes, people don't think there is any point in still being married. Maybe there are too many bad times. This is when divorce will most probably happen.

HANG IN THERE

Before you get a divorce, you are supposed to try to work things out (reconciliation). There are marriage guidance counsellors who try to help you do this. They say that it is best if couples are honest with each other and say what they think. Sometimes this is difficult in a divorce because people might be angry. Organisations like the Scottish Family Conciliation Service try to help. Some people do not think divorce is ever right. They say that when you get married you say you will stick together:

'Until death separates us.'

You are supposed to put up with the good times and the bad times and stay together. That is what marriage is about. That is why your **marriage vows** say:

'For richer, for poorer, in sickness and in health.'

Form of extract decree of divorce

EXTRACT DECREE OF DIVORCE

Sheriff Court   Court Ref No

Date of Decree   *In absence

Pursuer   Defender

Date of parties marriage   Place of parties marriage

The sheriff granted decree

(1) divorcing the defender from the Pursuer;

*(2) ordering that the following child(ren):

Full name(s)   Date(s) of birth

Reside with the *pursuer/defender and finding the *pursuer/defender entitled to be in contact with the following child(ren): as follows:

All in terms of the Children (Scotland) Act 1995.

*(3) ordaining payment
*(a) by the   to the   of a periodical allowance of £ per
*(b) by the   to the   of a capital sum of £
*(c) by the   to the   of £   per   as aliment for each child until that child attains years of age, said sum payable in advance and beginning at the date of this decree with interest thereon at the rate of per cent a year until payment;
*(d) by the   to the   of £ of expenses;

*(4) finding the   liable to the   in expenses as the same may be subsequently taxed.

This extract is warrant for all lawful execution hereon.

Date: (*insert date*)   Sheriff Clerk (depute)
*Delete as appropriate.

figure 3.6 *An extract decree of divorce*

THE 'COST' OF DIVORCE

Personal

Divorces take a long time. There are sometimes big arguments. These can be very emotional. When you have made a life together it is hard to take it apart and still be friends.

Family

If you have children, divorce is even more complicated. If the children are under 16, the court has to decide:

- Whether mum or dad will look after them (**custodial** rights).
- How much time they can spend with the parent they don't live with (right of **access**).
- Who should pay for their upbringing (support).

This sometimes leads to 'tugs of love'. Children usually find divorces difficult. Two people they love might not be behaving very nicely towards each other.

DISCUSSION POINT

Should mums always get to look after the children after divorce? What about dads?

CASE STUDY

In May 1974, two men started an organisation called 'Families need Fathers'. They thought it unfair that mothers usually get to look after the children. They thought that the children needed their dads too. They said that it is time we realised that children need both parents, even if they are not together any more.

Social

Some people think that having more single mums and dads is not good for society. They think it might mean that children do not get brought up as well as they might with two parents around. Other people think this isn't true at all. They say that as long as you love your children it doesn't matter whether there is a mum and dad always around or not. Also, divorced parents may be better than married ones who always fight.

MAKE IT EASY ON YOURSELF

Divorces can be sorted out in two years. As long as both partners agree. Some people think that divorce should not take as long because:

- It would stop it dragging on for ages.
- People can get on with their lives.

But others think:

- If it is too quick people might not think carefully enough.
- If people know they can get a quick divorce, they might not try too hard at being married.

DISCUSSION POINT

How long should you have to wait to get a divorce?

The fact that there are more divorces might mean that people don't think so much of marriage now. But it might also mean that people don't want to stick with failed relationships. Whether this is good or bad depends on what you think.

FACTS AND FIGURES

- The rate of divorce fell in Scotland between 1993 and 1998, but not for people who have been married more than 25 years. Their divorce rate went up by 35%.
- In 1998, 150,000 children went through a family divorce.
- Divorces cost society about £5 billion pounds every year.

Family Policy Studies Centre Report, March 2000

figure 3.7 *Marriage guidance counselling*

MORAL RESPONSES

CHRISTIANITY

Christians have different ideas about divorce. The major teaching is in Matthew 19:3–12:

What God has joined together, let no one separate. If you divorce your wife (unless she is unfaithful) you are being unfaithful.

The Roman Catholic Church does not agree with divorce. But your marriage can be ended (annulled). This can be done if you were never properly married in the first place.

In I Corinthians 7:10–16, Paul says that Jesus' teaching was right and you cannot divorce. But some Christians think that the Bible cannot make up its mind about divorce. So you can agree with divorce or not if you like.

You should try to be kind to people going through divorce. You should not judge them – that's not your job. Some say divorce is fine, because at least it is honest and lets people get on with their lives. In the Church of Scotland a minister can choose not to allow divorced people to re-marry in church.

Some Christians think your marriage vows are holy. You should never go back on them.

ISLAM

Muslims let people get divorced (talaq). But this should always be after you have tried everything to save your marriage. A man has to say 'I divorce you' three times (over three months). This is called the iddah.

It is more complicated for a woman to divorce her husband. She has to prove that there is a good reason for it. Muslims think it is very important to make sure the children are looked after if there is a divorce.

You can marry someone else after you have divorced. You can also re-marry the person you divorced if you like. You have got to leave some time between the divorce and the wedding. This is because if the woman is pregnant, no one can be confused about who the dad is.

You should try not to get divorced if you can (see Surahs 2:227–232; 65:1–7; 4:35). If your marriage does fail you should not suffer any more than you have to.

EGOISM

Egoists do not have a problem with divorce. They think you should be able to divorce as many times as you want. You want to make sure that you get a good deal out of divorce. A divorce between two Egoists could be horrible!

Egoists might want the children or not (not if they thought they were a pest!). They would not worry very much about the 'costs' of divorce to anyone else but themselves.

Mind you, if marriage means having to put up with someone else's ways, an Egoist might not like it much in the first place!

UTILITARIANISM

Utilitarians would think divorce is fine as long as it doesn't harm too many people. If you are in a failed marriage then there will be more pain than pleasure. So, you should get out of it.

But you might stay married for the sake of the children. If children of single parents have more problems this might be bad for society. The Utilitarian would not want that. This might mean that the Utilitarian would stick with a bad marriage. This would be to stop people suffering because of the divorce.

Maybe more divorces would weaken society. This would not be good.

Key Words

Access – How often you get to see the children if you haven't got custody.

Custody – Who gets the children.

Desertion – Leaving your husband/wife.

Divorce – A legal agreement separating a married couple.

Infidelity/adultery – Having a relationship with someone while you are married to someone else.

Marriage vows – Promises you make when getting married.

Separation – When a married couple agrees to split up.

Activities

Knowledge & Understanding

1 Write down **one** thing that the study on divorce showed.
2 Write **one** thing which might cause a divorce.
3 What is reconciliation?
4 How might divorce be more difficult for couples with children?
5 Do you think it should be easier or harder to get a divorce? Give **one** reason for your answer.
6 What does the Roman Catholic Church think of divorce?
7 Why might a divorce between two Egoists be 'horrible'?

Analysis

1 Copy and complete this true/false quiz.
  a Adultery is one cause of divorce.
  b Desertion means leaving your partner for one year.
  c Marriage guidance counsellors try to help people get divorced.
  d Custodial rights means who gets to look after the children after a divorce.
  e In 1998, 150,000 children went through a family divorce.
  f Muslims don't let you get divorced.
  g Egoists think if you want a divorce it is up to you.
2 Design a short information leaflet which could be given to children whose parents are getting divorced. Use the following headings. Choose which age group of children you would like it to be for.
  a What is a divorce?
  b Some reasons for people getting divorced
  c It is NOT YOUR FAULT
  d Questions you might have (and some answers)
  e What will happen to you now?
3 Some people think that there are more divorces nowadays because there are more pressures in life. In groups, make a list of what those pressures might be. Put them in order – worst first, next worst etc.
4 Try the following questionnaire with your class. Treat answers anonymously:
  a Do you think people should stay married no matter what?
  b What do you think would be most likely to make you want to divorce your husband/wife?
  c What problems do you think divorces can cause?

Evaluation

'Married couples should stick together for the sake of the children.'
Do you agree? Give **one** reason for your answer.

Assessment question

Outcome 2 (12) Copy and complete:
A religious person might think divorce is wrong because

____.

An Egoist might think divorce is wrong because

____.

A Utilitarian might think divorce is wrong because

____.

Homework

Ask as many people as you can this question:
At the moment, divorces can be sorted out in two years. Is this too long?

Extension work

Imagine you are the child in this situation.
You are 12 years old. Your parents have always got on well (you think). But they have been arguing a lot. You don't know why. One day they tell you that they are getting a divorce. You are confused.
Try to think about how you would feel. You can express this in any of these ways:

- A diary entry of the day they tell you.
- A letter/e-mail to your best friend.
- A piece of artwork that expresses how you feel.
- A letter to your parents.

4 HUMAN RIGHTS

CAPITAL PUNISHMENT

CASE STUDY

In February 2000, Jeffrey Dillingham was executed.

He had a final meal. He asked for (and got):

1 cheeseburger with American, cheddar and mozzarella cheese, without mayonnaise, mustard or onions, large French fries; bowl of macaroni and cheese; lasagne with 2 slices of garlic bread; 4 oz nacho cheese; 3 large cinnamon rolls; 5 scrambled eggs; 8 pints of chocolate milk.

Texas Department of Criminal Justice

He made a final statement. He said:

'I would like to apologise to the victim's family for what I did.' He thanked his own family for 'the good things' in his life.

Dallas Morning News, 11 February 2000

When you are killed in the electric chair your body throws itself against the straps that hold you. Your body changes colour. Your flesh swells. It might catch fire. You might wet yourself or throw up blood. People who watch this happen say they can smell burning skin.

When you are hanged, you are weighed. This weight is divided by 1260. This gives you the 'drop' in feet. This is supposed to kill you right away. It stops you being strangled. It stops your head being ripped off. The noose is put behind your left ear. This snaps your neck as you drop.

Amnesty International

WHAT IS IT FOR?

When you read about someone being executed, it is not very nice. Some think it is so horrible that it should not happen. Some think the people executed deserve it.

Capital punishment is when you are killed for your crimes. Usually it is when you have killed someone. The government orders your death. Does it have the right to? There is still capital punishment in lots of countries. It stopped in Britain in 1965.

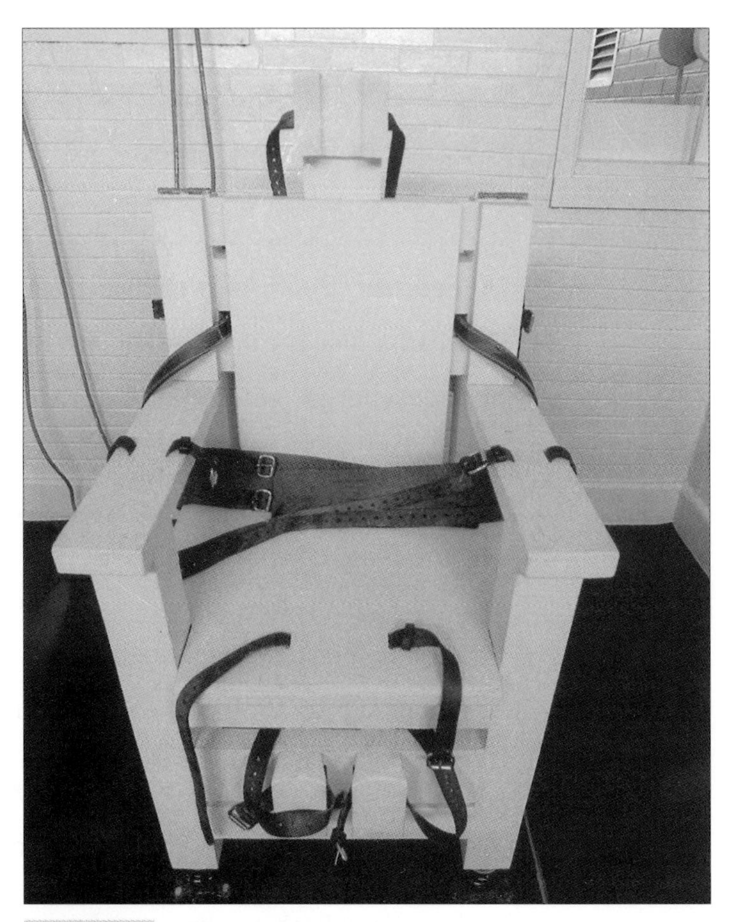

figure 4.1 *The electric chair*

WHOSE FAULT?

When someone has done something bad, is it just their fault? When someone has done something wrong, there is usually a reason. Sometimes these reasons are very complicated. Maybe the criminal was poor. Maybe he was treated badly when he was a child. People who disagree with capital punishment ask why most people who are executed are poor or **disadvantaged**? They say it is not just coincidence. If your life isn't good you are more likely to be a criminal. That is not only your fault, it is everybody's. Some don't agree with this. They say that we are all responsible for what we do. You can't blame others.

DISCUSSION POINT

Do you think we are all responsible for our own actions?

Here are some arguments in favour of capital punishment:

- Capital punishment puts people off crime. In the USA in 1960 there were 9140 murders. Capital punishment existed then. In 1975 they got rid of capital punishment (for a while). There were 20,510 murders. Capital punishment obviously puts people off crime.
- Capital punishment shows that society cares about crime. If a murderer is executed it shows that we care about his victim.
- It protects us. There is one less murderer roaming the streets.
- It is cheaper than keeping someone in prison for a long time.

Here are some arguments against capital punishment:

- You can make mistakes. What if you execute someone and then find new evidence? This proves they were not the killer. You can't bring the dead back and say sorry.
- How can you then say it is wrong to kill? Capital punishment is killing too. Most killers kill in anger. They don't think hard about it. Capital Punishment is cold and thoughtful. That is even worse. No wonder people are confused!
- When you are in prison you can change for the better. That is of no use if you are executed. Many killers do change in prison. They become better people. What is the point in killing them then?
- It does not put other people off crime.
- It is an easy way to deal with poor people. We should make their lives better. Then they might not want to kill.

CASE STUDY

In the 1970s and 1980s Jimmy Boyle was a Glasgow 'hard man'. He was in prison for murder. He spent lots of time in solitary confinement. The prison officers thought he was one of the most violent prisoners ever.

They put him into Barlinnie Special Unit. Instead of harsh treatment they tried to make him a better person. He found out he was good at art. He became a better person. They set him free. He now helps young people in Edinburgh. He doesn't want them to end up like he was. In some countries, Jimmy would have been executed.

THE VALUE OF LIFE

Capital punishment is a way of showing how wrong it is to kill. Some people think life is 'sacred'. This means it is special. No one should take anyone's life. Some people think you can take life if it is the best thing to do. Everybody has the right to life. If you kill someone maybe you give up your right to life. Some kinds of killing may be worse than others.

Some people say that capital punishment is better than life in prison. At least capital punishment is over quickly.

DISCUSSION POINT

Do you think capital punishment is worse than life in prison?

figure 4.2 *Death row cells*

FACTS AND FIGURES

- In the USA in 1999 there were 98 executions. This is about one every four days.
- In the USA you can be executed even if you are a child or you are mentally ill.
- There are at least seven ways people can be executed. These are all used in the world today: hanging; electric chair; guillotine; firing squad; gas chamber; lethal injection; stoning.

The point of being punished is:

- Punishment is **revenge** for what you have done. It pleases the victim's family if the criminal gets what they deserved. But, can anyone really be pleased about another death?
- Punishment should put you off doing the same crime again. This is called **deterrence**. But when someone is executed, they can't do the crime again. The idea is that capital punishment is so horrible you would never want

it to happen to you. So, you will not do anything which might get you capital punishment. People who are executed are an example for others: 'This could happen to you if you do what I've done'. This should put people off crime. Does it? Countries with capital punishment seem to have as much crime as countries where there is no capital punishment.

What do you think punishment is for?

- Punishment should help you learn to be good. You should come out of prison a better person. You should have learned your lesson. This is called **reformation.** It means you won't do the same crime again. But with capital punishment you never come out of prison alive.

MORAL RESPONSES

CHRISTIANITY

Some **Christians** strongly support capital punishment. In the Bible it says: '*eye for eye, tooth for tooth.*' (Exodus 21: 24-5).

Christians say this means that if you kill someone your life should be taken.

Other Christians say that this was written long ago. Things are different now. Then it was just a way to stop people taking revenge. Nowadays we should forgive and move on.

Jesus said:

'*You have heard it said, "eye for eye, tooth for tooth", but I tell you now. Do not take revenge on someone who does you wrong.*' (Matthew 5:38.)

Many Christians think capital punishment is wrong because it doesn't give someone the chance to change their ways. Everyone can. Capital punishment isn't forgiving. Christians should be.

ISLAM

Many **Muslims** think capital punishment is right. They say your punishment should be the same as your crime (Surah 16:126).

Punishment should also put other people off from committing the same crime. It should 'please' the family of your victim.

Muslims also think **mercy** is important. This means letting someone off. In some Muslim countries a victim's family can ask for the murderer not to be killed (see Surah 2:178).

Allah forgives us all for the wrong things we do. We should forgive others too.

EGOISM

The **Egoist** can support and oppose capital punishment. If he was a killer and going to be executed he might think:

- Even if you were doing life in prison you could still enjoy yourself sometimes. If you are executed, you can't enjoy yourself any more.
- At least death is quick. Life in prison might be one long misery.

If the Egoist was not a killer waiting to be executed he might think:

- It is good because it means there is one less killer about.
- It is good because it is cheaper.
- It is good because it might put people off killing.
- It is bad because you can't make mistakes. What if one day it was the Egoist on death row? What if the evidence was wrong?
- It is bad because it makes the world a nastier place. If we don't mind our government executing people, what will we let them do next?

UTILITARIANISM

In 1868 John Stuart Mill said capital punishment was good. He was a **Utilitarian**. He said that murder was so bad that a murderer should pay with his own life.

Death is quick. It is better than life in prison. That is even more miserable.

Mill said capital punishment didn't put people off crime. 'Hardened criminals' got used to the idea. It didn't stop them killing. But it might put someone off who wasn't a criminal yet.

Mill did not think that capital punishment was a funny way to show that killing was wrong. When someone has done something wrong they are put in prison. Putting them in prison is a sort of crime too! So, taking a killer's life is the same thing. No better, no worse.

A Utilitarian would say that capital punishment is good if it makes the world safer. But if it means that we don't care about life it is not good.

KEY WORDS

Capital punishment – Death penalty/state execution. Taking someone's life because they have carried out a crime.

Deterrence – Putting someone off from doing something.

Disadvantaged – When you do not have the same opportunities in life as other people.

Mercy – Letting someone off a crime as an act of kindness.

Reformation – Giving someone the chance to change for the better.

Revenge – Getting someone back for what they have done.

ACTIVITIES

Knowledge & Understanding

1 Can you think why Jeffrey Dillingham might have asked for all that food for his last meal?

2 Copy and complete:
Capital p_______________ is when you are killed for your crimes. It is usually for crimes where you have k________ someone.
The g________ orders your death.

3 Do the following crossword.

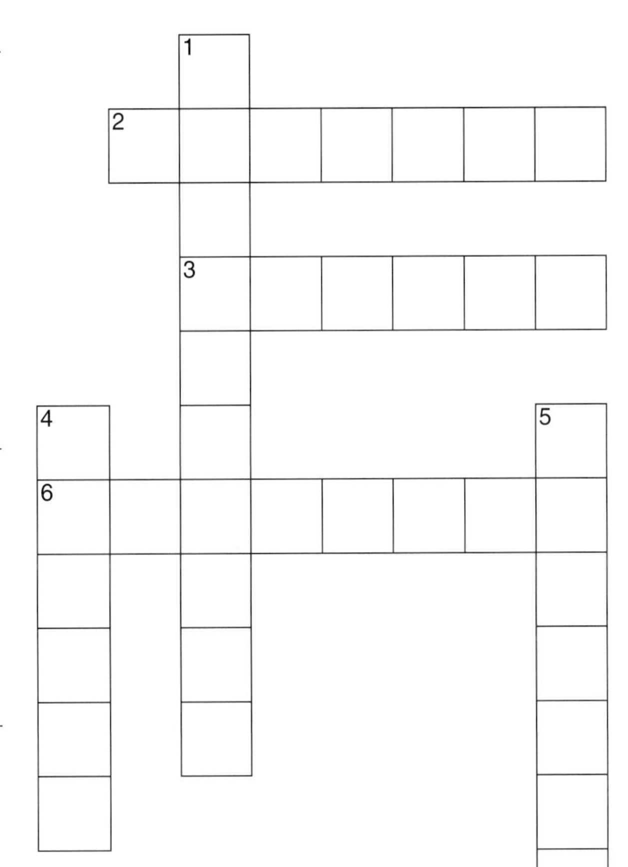

Across

2 Getting back at someone for something they have done wrong. (7)

3 When you are used to show others what will happen to them if they do the same. (7)

6 Another word for being put to death. (8)

Down

1 Putting you off doing something. (10)

4 When you are reformed you become a better one of these. (6)

5 The word used for when you have learned your lesson. (11)

4 Give **two** reasons why someone might commit a serious crime.

5 Some people think capital punishment *protects* us. What do they mean?

6 Here are **three** arguments against capital punishment. Reorder the words so the sentences make sense:

  a Killing a someone is funny way killing's wrong to show that.

  b Capital off crime doesn't put people punishment.

  c It is just way to deal the easy with poor people.

7 What do Christians mean by 'eye for eye'?

8 Give **one** reason why an Egoist might agree with capital punishment.

Analysis

1 Design a poster which is either for or against capital punishment.

2 You are in charge of a group which does not agree with capital punishment. Design an information leaflet explaining your views as follows:

Side 1: (outside)

WHAT CAN YOU DO?		Cover
• ________ • ________ • ________	Simple anti-capital punishment slogan on this page.	Your poster idea from Analysis Question 1

Side 2: (inside)

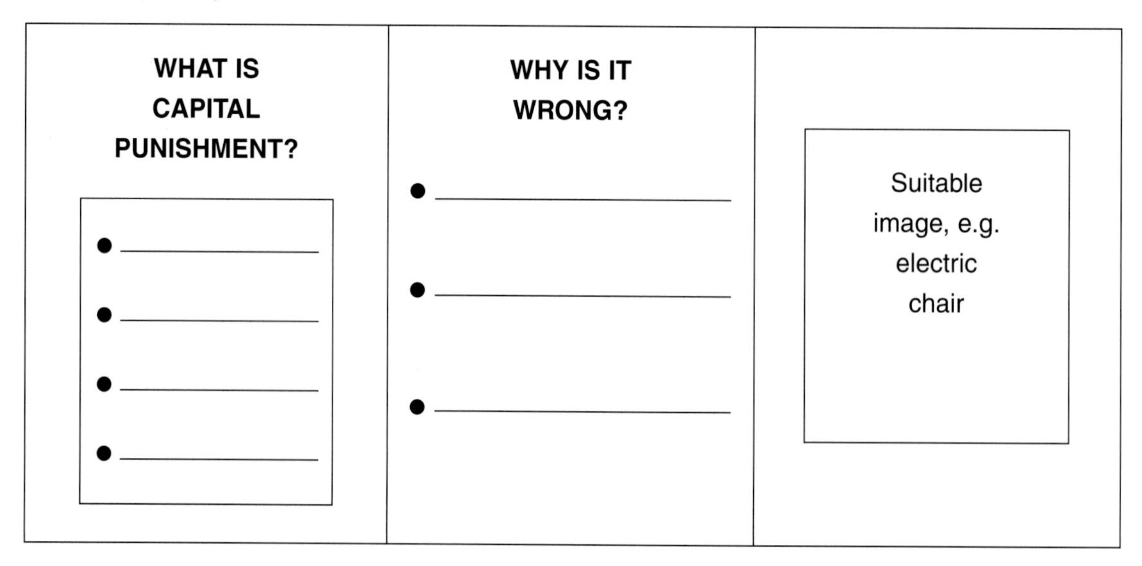

3 Carry out this questionnaire in your class/school.

a Do you think capital punishment is right?
Yes ☐ No ☐ Sometimes ☐
Comments ______________________.

b Do you think some crimes deserve capital punishment?
Yes ☐ No ☐ Don't Know ☐
Comments ______________________.

c Do you think they should bring capital punishment back in Britain?
Yes ☐ No ☐ Don't Know ☐
Comments ______________________.

Make a short report of your findings to the class.

4 In groups of four discuss this statement:
'Capital Punishment is always wrong.'
One of you should argue as if you were a Christian, one a Muslim, one an Egoist and one a Utilitarian.

Evaluation

'Capital Punishment is a strange way to show people that it is wrong to kill.'
Do you agree or not? Give at least **one** reason for your answer.

Assessment question

Outcome 2 (12) It has been decided to bring capital punishment back in Scotland. Writing one sentence for each, what might an Egoist, Utilitarian and Religious person say about that?

Homework

Use your questionnaire from Analysis question 3 on people at home. Then write the answer to this question:
Is there any difference between the views of adults and young people about capital punishment?

Extension work

1 Look in your school Library/Resource Centre or on the internet for information on capital punishment. Try to find:
a How many executions there have been in the last year worldwide.
b How most people are executed.
c What crimes people are executed for.
d Which country in the world carries out the most executions.

2 You have been asked to write a letter to someone on death row who is about to be executed. In this letter you have to explain your views on capital punishment. What would you say?

Answers to Knowledge and Understanding Question 3:
Across
1 Revenge. 2 Example. 3 Executed.
Down
2 Deterrence. 5 Person. 6 Rehabilitated.

RACIAL PREJUDICE

CASE STUDY

In December 1997, the government made it illegal to be anti-English. Maybe this was because they thought more Scottish people were being **anti**-English, setting up groups like 'Settler Watch'. This group thinks that English people are making Scotland too much like England. The group says it is not racist though. Some people think it is.

In the Borders, a pub owner said he was being hassled to leave town. He says it was because he's English.

Is it racist for Scots to be anti-English?

PREJUDICE

This is when you judge someone before you know much about them. You might decide you don't like them because of their skin colour. The Scottish Ethnic **Minorities** Research Unit interviewed 150 people in Glasgow. They were Indian, Pakistani or Chinese:

120 had been called racist names.

30 had been attacked.

75 had their homes damaged.

All over the world there seem to be problems of **racism**. In some countries, there have been wars. In these wars, different racial or **ethnic groups** have tried to get rid of each other. This is called 'ethnic cleansing'.

WHAT IS BEHIND RACIAL PREJUDICE?

- When things are going wrong some people like to blame others. It is easy to blame someone who is different to you. Especially if there are more of 'you' than 'them'. When you use people this way this is called making them a **scapegoat**.
- If you aren't very happy with yourself you might take this out on others. Maybe you have a rotten job or a sad social life. Being racist might give you a feeling of power.

figure 4.3 *A Scottish sikh*

DISCUSSION POINT

Do you know of any racial stereotypes? Are they true?

- When you are racist you don't need to know the facts. You just treat everyone in a racial group the same. This is called **stereotyping**. You ignore that everyone is different. After all, not all Scots eat haggis do they?

EXPLANATION OR EXCUSE?

Most people don't agree with racism. Especially when it leads to violence. Some people have tried to explain it:

- You are more likely to survive when you are part of a group. Sometimes this group is based on race. The trouble is this makes it more likely for different groups to clash. When groups keep to themselves it makes racism more probable.
- Racism is likely to happen when people's lives aren't good. When people are poor or miserable, they will look around for someone to blame. People like Hitler used this fact in the Second World War to turn people against the Jews.

- Sometimes people are racist because that is how they have been brought up. They need to be re-educated.
- Some people think they should be racist to protect their own 'way of life'. People are a bit scared of anything different. It is too easy to think of someone different as a threat.
- In trying to protect your own way of life you might end up being 'racist' yourself. For example, if you don't let people marry outside your race. Some people might think this gives them good reason to be racist against you.
- Racism might be going along with the crowd. Some people might not really think about it, but are racist because other people are.

Which of these do you think is an explanation, and which is an excuse?

THE DAMAGE

Racism causes pain. This can be physical or mental. It makes people feel bad about themselves. It makes the world less safe for everyone. Maybe racism is so bad because it is based on something you cannot change. You can't help how you were born. Anyway, who wants a world where everyone is the same?

figure 4.4 *Groups like these may believe they are 'only protecting their own way of life'*

FACTS AND FIGURES

- One of the first members of 'Settler Watch' was German.
- An event to celebrate differences was held in Glasgow in September 2000. This was called 'Threads in the Tartan'.
- About 1.25% of Scottish people are 'non-white'.

RESPONDING TO RACISM

- Groups like the Anne Frank Institute in Amsterdam try to teach people about the harm racism can do.
- Mahatma Gandhi responded to racism with non-violent action.
- Martin Luther King did this too. He achieved many good things for black Americans. But he was killed by his enemies.
- Malcolm X had a different idea. He said people should reply to racism with violence.
- Nelson Mandela spent many years in prison in South Africa. He tried to get equal rights for blacks. He was successful. He became South Africa's President.
- In the UK there are organisations which watch out for racism. For example, the Commission for Racial Equality. There are laws against racism in the UK too.

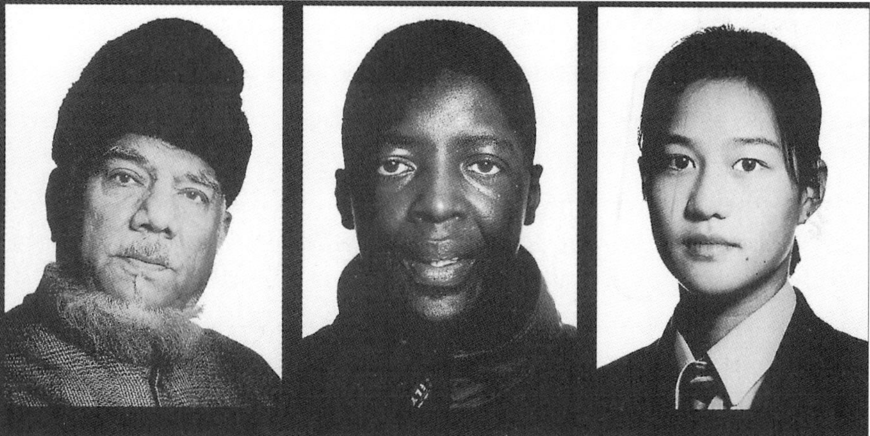

figure 4.5 Anti-racist campaign poster

DISCUSSION POINT

What do you think of this poster?

MORAL RESPONSES

CHRISTIANITY

Christians believe that God made everyone just like him (Genesis 1:26).

This means you cannot be racist because everyone is like God.

The story of the Good Samaritan is a story showing that racism is wrong. Jesus shows that you should help people even if you don't like them. Even if they are very different to you.

Jesus said you should 'love others' as much as you love yourself.

St Paul says that everyone is equal (Galatians 3:28). You should treat everyone in the same way because they are just as important to God as you are.

All of this means that a Christian should not be racist.

ISLAM

Muslims believe that Allah made everyone. So everyone deserves respect. The only difference between people is how much faith they have.

The Qur'an seems to say that variety is a good thing. All humans are part of one family. It does not matter where you are from or what colour you are.

During the Hajj, every Muslim dresses in the same way. This shows that everyone is equal. Muslims should treat everyone equally, especially those who have faith in God.

In Britain, Muslims are a minority. They are more likely to suffer from racism than to be racist. Muslims should not act in a racist way, but when people are nasty to them they should, 'reply back with mild words of peace' (Surah 25:63).

EGOISM

An **Egoist** might think racism is fine. If racism kept minorities out of a job then he or she could get the job. There is no point in treating people as equals if there is no benefit to you.

He or she might be racist to protect his own way of life. Being racist might mean he can blame others for his own problems.

If an Egoist was in a minority group he or she might use racism for his own good. He might say that people are being racist when they aren't.

But if racism makes society less stable, the Egoist might not like it.

UTILITARIANISM

A **Utilitarian** might have problems with racism.

Utilitarians think that what is best is what does most good for most people (the majority). This might mean that minorities get a hard time. They come second. But this might cause unhappiness. The Utilitarian would not like that.

So, the Utilitarian has to balance things. A Utilitarian would not be directly racist. This would make society as a whole bad. But sometimes a Utilitarian choice might mean that you cannot avoid racism. Trying to get the best for the most might mean others get a bad deal.

KEY WORDS

Anti – When you are against something or someone (e.g. anti-English means not liking the English).

Ethnic group – A smaller group in a larger society. Made up of people who have the same religion, culture or language etc.

Minority – A smaller group within a larger one (e.g. Asians in Scotland).

Racism – Prejudice which is based on the colour of someone's skin, or where they come from.

Scapegoat – A person or group who gets the blame for something they didn't do.

Stereotype – A mixture of things which makes up a typical example of something (e.g. all Scots are mean with their money).

ACTIVITIES

Knowledge & Understanding

1 What do the people in 'Settler Watch' think?

2 Do this true/false quiz.
- a Prejudice means judging people before you know much about them.
- b Racism is not a kind of prejudice.
- c A minority is a small group in a larger society.
- d A scapegoat is someone or something you can blame.
- e All Scots eat haggis.
- f Sometimes people are racist because that is how they were brought up.
- g Some people are racist because they just go along with the crowd.

3 Name **one** problem racism can bring.

4 Give **one** reason why a Christian should not be racist.

5 Why might an Egoist be racist?

Analysis

1 What does it mean to be Scottish? In your class ask the following questions. You may like to write these out and have them returned anonymously.
- a Were you born in Scotland?
- b Were your parents born in Scotland?
- c Were your grandparents born in Scotland?
- d How long have you lived in this country?
- e Can you speak English?
- f Can you speak Gaelic?
- g Do you know what the Doric is?

- **h** Can you name six famous Scots who are no longer living?
- **i** How many Kings and Queens of Scotland can you name?
- **j** What are the ingredients for haggis?

2 Prepare a display board for your classroom which shows examples of racism in Scotland. You should use magazine and newspaper items.

3 Write down **three** things your school does to help stop racism. Write down **five** things it should do.

4 Find out about Gandhi, Martin Luther King or Nelson Mandela. Write a report about them based on outline below. Your report should be about 100 words long.
- **a** Where and when did he live?
- **b** What was he fighting against?
- **c** What did he do?
- **d** How successful was he?

5 There has been a racist murder in your town. People have been asked by the local newspaper to add one sentence to an anti-racist wall which is in the town centre. This sentence should say why racism is wrong. Make up an anti-racist wall like this in your class. Everyone in the class should write their own sentence. You should also think of what might be written by a Christian, Muslim, Egoist and Utilitarian. You could add 'their' sentence to your wall.

Evaluation

'Racism is always wrong.'
Say whether you agree or not and give **one** reason for your answer.

Assessment question

Outcome 3 (11) 'Racists are only protecting their own way of life.'
Do you agree? Give **two** reasons for your answer.

Homework

Make a list of **three** things the Scottish parliament could do to stop racism.

Extension work

1 You must organise an event in your town. The point of the event is to try to stop people being racist.
Where would you have this event?
When?
What might be in it?
Draw up a plan for the event.

2 Someone in your class is telling racist jokes. You have been asked to get them to stop. How might you explain to them that this is wrong?

FREEDOM OF SPEECH

CASE STUDY

Around 12th July every year there are Orange Marches. Members of the Orange Lodge parade in Scotland's streets.These marches can be seen as celebrating a way of life. They can also be seen as prejudice. In Northern Ireland, there are the Drumcree Marches.There can be serious trouble at these marches. Each local authority has to decide whether these marches can happen or not.The police give them advice. Some people think these marches should be banned.They say they just make wrong views look as if they're right.

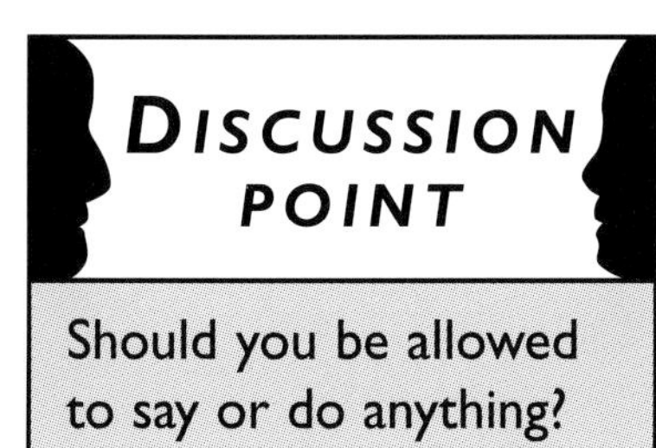

Should you be allowed to say or do anything?

figure 4.6 *Orange March parade*

I CAN DO ANYTHING

Should you be allowed to say and do anything you want? Or should you have to keep some things to yourself? How free should people be to say or do anything?

If your school lets you on the internet it probably controls what sites you can get on to. Some say the whole Internet should be controlled. This is to stop dodgy people looking at dodgy sites. Others say this is taking away your freedom. **Censorship** is when you are not allowed certain things. What things are usually censored?

Pornography

You can show lots of things in a film or magazine. But in Britain, it is against the law to show a man's erect penis. Films and magazines are checked. They are then given a rating. This shows who can see them. For example, a film with an 18 rating should not be seen by anyone under 18 years old. Sex with animals or children is illegal and it is banned from magazines and films. If there is violent sex, that might be banned too. TV is censored as well. Certain things can only be shown after 9 p.m. This is called the **watershed.**

Violence

Only so much violence is allowed on TV or in films.

Freedom to express your views

You cannot say anything about anyone. There are laws to stop you. These are called **libel** laws. But in Britain you are allowed to express your opinion. In some countries you are not.

Propaganda

Sometimes information is censored. In a war your government might not tell the whole truth. This is to stop people thinking things are going badly. It's also to make sure some things stay secret.

Other 'unacceptable' views

Sometimes people are not allowed to say what they think. Sometimes this is because people speak against the government. In Britain you are allowed to speak out against the government if you want. In some countries you are not allowed to. In some countries you also have to dress or behave in a certain way. In Britain people think you should be careful what you say. For example, most people think it would be wrong to make fun of people because they are disabled.

Who should decide what is censored?

figure 4.7 *A propoganda poster from World War II*

THE VALUE OF CENSORSHIP?

- It should protect everyone. If you could do anything the world would be a dangerous place.
- Maybe you should not be allowed to see anything you want. Maybe you are 'weak' and will be influenced by what you see. Perhaps seeing violence in a film will make you more violent. You should be protected from this. Possibly people who have dangerous ideas should be censored. Maybe racists should not be allowed to say what they think in public.
- You should be careful what you say. Perhaps it could harm someone. Once you have said it you can't take it back.
- Some people think things like pornography take advantage of people. Censorship stops this.
- Censorship stops people copying things which are wrong. If you see it on TV you might be more likely to do it yourself.
- Censorship means that everyone knows what is right and what is wrong. It stops views getting across which might cause harm. This makes life safer for everyone.

NO CENSORSHIP

- People should be able to make their own decisions. You can switch off your TV if you don't like what you see. Anyway, who makes these decisions?
- There is no proof that banning things makes people any better. There is just as much violence in countries where TV violence is censored.
- If you do ban things they don't go away. It might make it harder to control things properly.
- Sometimes it is good to criticise things like the government. It keeps them on their toes. If you try to ban people's opinions, you might make them stronger.

DISCUSSION POINT

If you ban something, do you just make it worse?

Badly behaved children might be copying what they see on TV. The Independent Television Commission (ITC) says that characters on TV like Bart Simpson might make children watching behave like him.

Times Educational Supplement, 10 November 2000 (adapted)

figure 4.8 *South Park characters. Do you think characters in cartoons like this can influence people's behaviour?*

MORAL RESPONSES

CHRISTIANITY

Christians believe that certain things should be banned. This is a good way of protecting weak people. You should care for others (Romans 13:9). This sometimes means that we should help people to not do certain things. You should set a good example. This might mean censoring bad examples.

But Christians believe that you should speak out against things which are wrong. This might mean going against the government. The government should be there to protect everyone. So Christians might have a problem. They should support the government but only if they think it is doing good (Matthew 22:15–22). The Old Testament prophets were always complaining about the government. So Christians should do so too.

However, Jesus taught people to make up their own minds about things. So maybe we should do this about censorship.

ISLAM

Muslims should be against injustice. It doesn't matter who is carrying it out. A Muslim might have to remind the government what is right.

Muslims also think it is important to help each other to do what is right. This might mean protecting people from seeing some things.

In Islam, women should be covered. This protects them. It also stops men having bad thoughts. Some think this is censorship. Muslims say it is a way of helping people to be good. Muslims say that people in the west have too much freedom. They say that pornography is an example of this. You should not be able to say anything you want because it might harm or insult others. The Salman Rushdie case is an example.

EGOISM

An **Egoist** could take two views:

- Usually Egoists like complete freedom. They want to say and do whatever they want. No one else should stop you doing or seeing what you want.
- But if censorship protects you then it is good. For example, if watching violence on TV makes you violent, it is bad. If the Egoist is attacked by someone who has seen violence on TV, he might want violence censored. Not everyone should have freedom of choice if that means problems for the Egoist.

UTILITARIANISM

Utilitarians think freedom is very important. People will not be happy when everything they see or do is 'watched over' by someone else.

But Utilitarians would agree with censorship if it made the world a safer place. If TV violence leads to more real-life violence then maybe TV should be controlled. Censorship might protect the majority. Even though it harms the freedom of the minority. Maybe sometimes people have to have decisions made for them. Perhaps this is the only way to make sure that everyone benefits. Utilitarians would also agree that the government should support the interests of the majority. Sometimes this might mean clamping down on some people's freedom.

KEY WORDS

Censorship – When something is banned, usually for the good of others.

Influence – Where you are affected by what you see or read. Sometimes it might make you copy bad behaviour.

Libel – Saying something about someone which might cause them harm.

Watershed – A time before which you cannot show certain things. (9 p.m. in Britain).

ACTIVITIES

Knowledge & Understanding

1 What happens in Scotland around 12th July? Why do some people think this is wrong?
2 Write down **one** thing you are not allowed to see on British TV or in a film.
3 In your own words, write **one** reason for censorship and **one** reason against it.
4 Do you think people copy things they see on TV?
5 Why do Christians think censorship is sometimes a good thing?
6 Why do Muslim women cover themselves up? Do you think this is censorship?
7 Copy and complete, using the right choice of *italic* word:
Censorship is when you *ban/finish* certain things. Some people think it is a good idea. This is because it might stop people *copying/liking* what they see. Some people don't agree. They think it takes away your own *ideas/freedom*.

Analysis

1 Put the following headings into your workbook. For each one, think of **three** TV programmes which might match up with the heading:
- **a** These programmes might be racist
- **b** These programmes might contain swearing
- **c** These programmes might be offensive to women
- **d** These programmes show too much violence

2 Think of **two** TV programmes which people may think should be banned. Name them and say why people could think they should be banned. Do you think they should?
3 Try this questionnaire out in your class. After you have done this, see if you think there is any link between watching violent TV/films and being violent.

a How often do you watch TV programmes or films which contain violence?
- ☐ Every day.
- ☐ Once or twice a week.
- ☐ Only sometimes.
- ☐ Never.

b In the average year, how often do you:
- ☐ Hit someone?
- ☐ Shout at someone?
- ☐ Lose your temper?

4 In pairs, think of **three** rules that should be followed when the internet is used by these people:
A 7 year-old girl.
A 13 year-old boy.
A 38 year-old man.
A 26 year-old man who has been in prison for serious assault.
5 You are religious and so is your girlfriend (you are both 18). She has decided to get photographed for a pornographic magazine. Act out the discussion you might have.

Evaluation

'All violence on TV should be banned.' Do you agree with this? Give **one** reason for your answer.

Assessment question

Outcome 2 (11) Your local shop has decided to start selling pornographic magazines. There is a petition going round the houses asking for people to speak out against this. What might an Egoist and religious person think? Would they sign the petition? What reasons might they give for their choice? For each person write **one** sentence they might say about this.

Homework

In your own school, find out what kinds of websites you are not allowed to go on. Make a list of the types of sites you cannot access.

Extension work

1 A book which some people find offensive has been banned. Complete the following table:

Banning this book is good because:	**Banning this book is bad because:**
•	•
•	•
•	•

In each column write **three** reasons.

2 Imagine if the government decided that all kinds of censorship were wrong. It decided that nothing should be banned. Can you think of **three** problems this might cause?

5 War and Peace

Non-violence and pacifism

Case Study

The organisation Peace One Day is asking people all over the world to stop fighting for one day each year on 21st September. This day is called the UN International Day of Peace. Even if your country isn't at war you can still do something on this day to show that you want peace in our world.

Jeremy Gilley, who is running Peace One Day, has made a film about the campaign. This film shows young people all over the world talking about peace. Jeremy wants everyone to see this film. The film will be sent to all world governments to persuade them to stop fighting in wars for this one day. Jeremy believes that one day of world peace is possible if we all work together. To find out more, visit the website: www.peaceoneday.org

Philosophical pacifism

Some people think it is always wrong to fight in a war. Pacifism means refusing to be violent. **Pacifists** do not fight. Especially in wars. In 1914 there was an organisation called the Fellowship of Peace. This helped people who did not want to fight in the First World War. These people were called **conscientious objectors.** Sometimes they were put in prison. This was because they would not go and fight when the government told them to. Some people thought they were cowards.

By the time of the Second World War people were kinder to conscientious objectors. But in the USA, 6000 conscientious objectors were sent to prison. Some went to war, but they did not fight. They could help the wounded and do other jobs. This is called being a non-combatant.

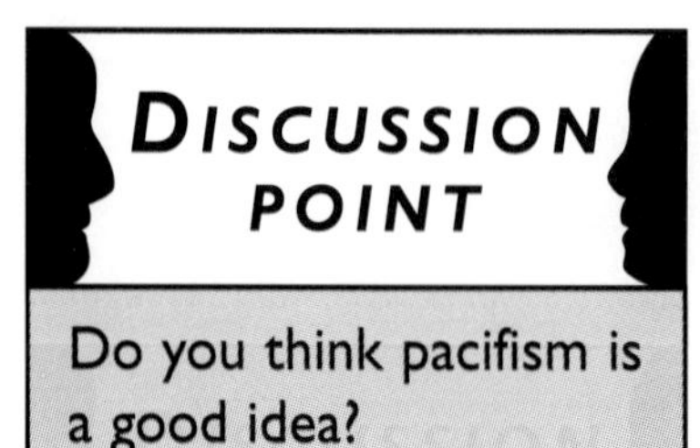

Do you think pacifism is a good idea?

Why might someone be a Pacifist?

- War is wrong. It is always wrong to kill.
- Wars don't help anyone. There are better ways to sort out arguments between countries.

figure 5.1 *Kofi Annan, Secretary-General, United Nations, and Jeremy Gilley, founder of Peace One Day*

RELIGIOUS PACIFISM

Many Christians think Jesus was against war. He taught people to love each other. You cannot be very loving in a war. Quakers are Christians. They think war is against the Bible. It is also something that has 'gone wrong' with people. Quakers think you should not fight back – even if this means you will die.

figure 5.2 *Anti-war demonstration*

Jesus told people to 'turn the other cheek'. This means if someone hits you, you don't hit them back. Quakers take this seriously.

Many Buddhists are pacifists. They think you should not harm any living thing. In the Vietnam war some Buddhists showed how wrong they thought the war was. They burned themselves to death in protest.

IDEAL OR IDEALISM?

Most people don't like war. But how do you avoid it? Pacifists say:

- Pacifism sets a good example for others. There are better ways to stop violence.
- War just means you made one choice and not another. War doesn't *have* to happen.
- Wars are complicated. But there is always a way to avoid war. You can talk things out.
- You should not use war as a threat. This is wrong. It will make people annoyed. They are then more likely to want to fight.

What would be good and bad about being a pacifist?

Some people think pacifists are wrong. They say:

- You cannot do nothing if you are under attack.
- Some world leaders are so bad that the only thing they understand is violence.
- Another country will only attack yours if they think they can get away with it. And they will if you won't fight back.
- Pacifism is a nice idea. But it doesn't work in real life.

NON-VIOLENT PROTEST

There is a nuclear submarine base at Faslane in Scotland. There is a camp next to it. This is called a peace camp. The people in this camp are protesters. They think that the base should be closed. One protester said:

We are here to remind people about the weapons in this base. They could kill millions of people. Having them is wrong. We're protesting peacefully. We don't believe in violence. Violent protest doesn't work.

figure 5.3 *Peace Camp at Faslane nuclear base*

What is non-violence?

This is a way of protesting. But you don't use violence. One of the peace groups at Faslane is called, 'Adomnan of Iona'. This is what they think non-violent protest is:

- Action – to get newspapers interested in the cause.
- Strikes and refusing to buy certain goods.
- Stopping things happening, like sitting on the road to stop traffic.
- Showing people different ways to do things.
- Marching and demonstrating in public.

DISCUSSION POINT

Which of these ways of non-violent protest do you think is the best?

The need for protest

People who agree with non-violent protest say:

- Sometimes it is the only thing you can do.
- You should be free to do it.

Facts and Figures

- 528,000 soldiers have done duty for the United Nations. They have tried to keep the peace. This has cost about $8.3 billion. 800 have died in battle.
- On 1 August 2000, 83 protesters were arrested at Faslane.
- Glasgow's Lord Provost welcomed a peace march into Glasgow the day after the arrests.

- Sometimes it is the only way to get heard. You can also speak for things which cannot speak – like animals.
- If lots of people protest, governments will listen.
- Some things are so bad we should complain about them.

The only thing that has ever changed the world is a small group of people who care enough.

Margaret Mead (adapted)

No need for protest

Some people think protesting is wrong. They say:

- You don't need to protest. You just vote against the government if you don't agree with it.
- People use protests to have a fight. They are a bad way to show what you think.
- Protests don't change anything. They annoy the government. Governments stick to their guns even more.

Moral responses

Christianity

Jesus taught **Christians** that peace was best. He lived in a country ruled by the Romans. Many people in the country thought the Romans should be kicked out. They wanted to go to war with the Romans. Some were waiting for God to send someone to lead them in this war. This leader would be called the Messiah. Many thought Jesus was the Messiah. But he was against war. Jesus was crucified. On the cross he asked God to forgive the people who were killing him. It seems that he does not think much of violence.

Jesus said that God likes people who try to bring peace. But Jesus was also kind to a Roman soldier. He did not ask the soldier to give up his job.

Christians think that we should be like Jesus. We should be peaceful. This is not always easy.

Islam

Muslims should protect their beliefs. Peace is best. But Muslims think that sometimes you have to go to war. Sometimes there is no choice.

You should not hit back, but be gentle if someone is nasty to you.

Muslims think there are times when you have to fight. The strong should protect the weak. You cannot do this if you are strong but won't fight.

Muslims think Allah brings peace, but that sometimes people do not.

EGOISM

Egoists usually prefer peace. War is dangerous after all.

An Egoist could be a pacifist. This would be a good excuse for him. He would not have to go to war.

Egoists might not want to be conscientious objectors and stay at home. They might get hassled. People might think they are scared to fight. They might go to war to help but not to fight.

If Egoists made weapons they might think war is a great idea. They could sell more weapons.

Egoists would support war if it protected them.

UTILITARIANISM

Utilitarians don't think war brings much pleasure. You would think they would always be against war. Wrong. Utilitarians also think freedom is important. It brings you lots of happiness. You might have to fight for your freedom.

War might be the only way to stop a country doing bad things. Even though war is bad – there are things which are worse. War costs a lot. People suffer and die. But once the war is won maybe the good things outweigh the bad.

KEY WORDS

Conscientious objector – Someone who refuses to fight in a war.

Non-violence – When you protest against something but do not use violence.

Pacifist – Someone who believes that fighting is wrong.

ACTIVITIES

Knowledge & Understanding

1 What is the organisation Peace One Day trying to do?
2 What is a conscientious objector?
3 Complete the table, putting the following statements in the right column:

A religious person might say this	An Egoist might say this	A Utilitarian might say this

- It is wrong to kill.
- War does not solve problems.
- The best way to deal with violence is peacefully.
- Some world leaders only understand violence.
- War is a way for the strong to protect the weak.
- If you don't fight back people will take advantage of you.

4 Write down **two** ways of carrying out a non-violent protest.
5 Copy and complete the sentences, using **one** of the statements listed:
 a Some Christians think war is wrong. This is because ____________
  - Jesus taught us to love each other.
  - War causes suffering.
  - War is boring.

 b Muslims think peace is best. They also think you sometimes have to go to war. This is because ____________
  - It is fun.
  - The strong have to protect the weak.
  - You might need to protect your beliefs.

 c Egoists would prefer not to go to war. This is because ____________
  - They have got better things to do.
  - They might get hurt.
  - They would not know where the war was.

Analysis

1 You are at a meeting with some of the world's leaders. They ask you to come up with four good reasons why they should give up war for one day. In pairs, come up with **four** reasons. Swap these with another pair. Find one of the other pair's reasons that you disagree with. Write why.
2 You disagree with something which is going on in your school. You decide to have a non-violent protest. You gather your friends to explain this to them. Write what you would say to them to:
 a Explain what a non-violent protest is.
 b Explain what you are going to do in your protest.
3 Imagine you are someone who has just heard the conversation between Jesus and the Roman soldier. You don't like the Romans. When you get home you tell your friends and family what you have heard. What would you say to them? Why would you be shocked by Jesus' actions?
4 Perhaps you have seen some posters that were used during the world wars to persuade people to fight for their country (ask your history department). Make up a poster in this style to persuade people to be conscientious objectors.

Evaluation

'Pacifism is silly.'
Do you agree? Give at least **one** reason for your answer.

Assessment question

Outcome 3 (11) Your country is at war. You get a letter. This letter tells you to go and join the army or you will be put in prison. What would you do?

Homework

You are a conscientious objector. You have been sent to prison because you will not go to war. Your 10 year-old son is ashamed of you. Write him a short letter explaining why you have made this choice.

Extension work

1. You are one of the world leaders in Analysis question 1. You think that to stop fighting your enemies for even one day is silly. How would you politely explain this to the Peace One Day organisation?
2. You are one of the world leaders in Analysis question 1. You think that to stop fighting your enemies for one day is a very good idea. How would you politely explain this to your government when you go home?
3. Make a list of jobs someone could do in a war without having to fight.

THE JUST WAR THEORY

CASE STUDY

I am a minister. I work for the Royal Navy. They call me a chaplain.

I'm not allowed to have a gun. In a battle I'm not allowed to fight. Instead, I help with the wounded.

How can I be a Christian when I help people who kill others?

These soldiers need God too. Sometimes it's hard for them. They see a lot of death. I don't think God likes war. I'm sure it makes him sad. But sometimes wars have to happen.

Sometimes the soldiers think God has forgotten about them. I'm there to show he hasn't.

A JUST WAR?

The **chaplain** thinks that war is a part of life. There have always been wars. But even in war there are rules. A man called Thomas Aquinas lived about 800 years ago. He came up with some rules about war. These rules are called the 'just war theory'.

A NEED FOR RULES?

Why might it be good to have rules in a war?

- Rules can stop the war getting bigger (escalating). They might stop other countries getting into the war.
- When the war is over people might be angry. The enemy could have done bad things during the war. You might want **revenge** on your enemies. If there were rules the enemy may not have been able to do such bad things. Then you would not need to get revenge.
- The rules might say you should fight fairly. If you don't then you could go to prison after the war. For example, you should not kill children in a war. If you do you could be accused of their murder after the war.

Some people think there should not be rules. You should do your best to win the war. How you win doesn't matter.

Do you think it is a good idea to have rules in war?

figure 5.4 *A naval battle off the coast of Vietnam, during the Vietnam War*

THE CONDITIONS FOR A JUST WAR

The just war theory has two parts:

- When you can (and cannot) go to war.
- What you can (and cannot) do in a war.

There has to be a good reason for the war

What is a good reason? People have different ideas. Most people think you should only fight to defend yourself. But you might want to strike first because this is the best way to defend yourself.

War must be a last resort

This means that you should have tried everything else. But that is not easy. How long do you talk with your enemies? They might be getting their armies ready while you are talking. Then they have got a better chance of winning than you.

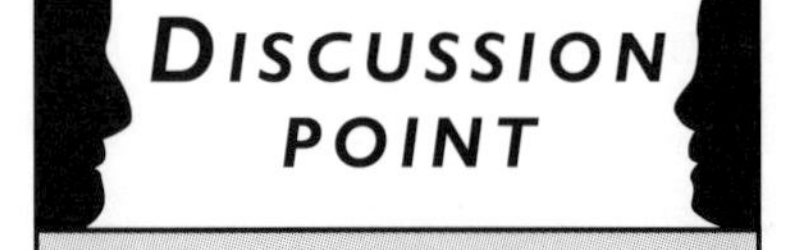

Do you think there are any good reasons for going to war?

The war should get rid of evil and replace it with good

It is difficult in war to say who is bad and who is good. Some people think it is obvious. But usually it is not.

What could governments do instead of going to war?

The war should be balanced

This is called **proportionality**. It means you should do what you need to do and then stop. You should decide what has to be done and then not go any further. If you do go further, you might cause more problems than you solve.

This is sometimes hard to do. In wars, people lose their cool. They can go too far. This can mean problems later.

Should you be allowed to kill anyone in the enemy's country?

You should try not to kill civilians

A **civilian** is anyone who is not a soldier. Civilian can also mean anyone who is not part of the war. You should not directly attack civilians. But who is a civilian? Some people think that everyone who lives in the enemy's country is the enemy. Whether they are all fighting or not. Civilians might not be fighting, but they may be helping the soldiers in other ways.

Only the government can start the war

What if you don't agree with the government? What if the government is a bit dodgy? What if the people in a country don't support their government?

Do other countries have the right to step in? Or should they mind their own business?

figure 5.5 *Bombing in Yugoslavia*

THEORY INTO ACTION

There are rules for war. Many countries in the world agree with these rules.

The Geneva Convention (1864)

This is an agreement between countries. It has been written down. It says things like, 'prisoners of war should be well treated'. It helps governments and armies know what they can and cannot do.

The Red Cross and the Red Crescent

These are international organisations. They try to help countries keep the Geneva **Convention**. They help the wounded in battle. If they are flying their flags, armies are not supposed to attack them.

There are other groups who help too, like Médecins Sans Frontières.

All of these organisations try to make sure that people treat each other as fairly as they can. Even in war.

FACTS AND FIGURES

- Since 1945, 14.9 million land mines have been found in Poland. These were left behind after the Second World War.
- Between 1945 and 1989, about 2 million people have been killed in wars.
- In the Gulf War in 1991, 100,234 people died.

MORAL RESPONSES

CHRISTIANITY

Some **Christians** think war is wrong. Some Christians think war is right. In the Old Testament, God helps the Israelites. Sometimes he helps them win battles. So some Christians think war is fine if you are fighting against evil.

Jesus said you should not fight violence with violence. He said you should 'love your enemies' (Matthew 5:44).

Once Jesus was very angry and threw people out of a holy building. He thought they were spoiling God's house (John 2:15). Some Christians think this means you can be violent if there is a good reason.

ISLAM

Some people think **Muslims** like war. When the Muslim faith started there were lots of battles. Muhammed himself fought a mighty battle at Badr. People thought he was winning the battles because Allah was on his side.

Muslims believe in *Jihad*. Sometimes this is called 'holy war'.

Only a religious leader can start a Jihad and it must be either:

- to defend Muslim beliefs.
- to get rid of bad leaders; or
- to bring freedom and protect the weak.

You should try not to start war. However, Muslims believe you should defend yourself if you need to.

Egoism

An **Egoist** would probably like to have rules in war. You would want the government to avoid war if possible. If your country went to war, rules might protect you.

An Egoist might think rules were a pest. He would just want his side to win. Who cares how they do it? No point in keeping rules if that means you lose.

Utilitarianism

Utilitarians have problems. Wars mean suffering. Not going to war might mean even more suffering.

War is a way for the strong to protect the weak. If you don't help them, many could die. So even though war is bad, there is sometimes no choice. You have to weigh things up. It might be better to go to war than not to.

Rules are good. They stop people taking revenge after the war. If they do keep taking revenge it is bad. It means that the war does not really end.

The Utilitarians have to be sure that going to war is for the best in the long run. They have to believe that it is the best for most people for the longest time.

Key Words

Chaplain – Usually a Christian minister who works for the armed forces (Royal Navy, Army, Royal Air Force).

Civilian – Someone who is not a member of the armed forces.

Convention – An agreement made between countries.

Last resort – When you have tried everything else.

Proportionality – Doing what you meant to do and no more.

Revenge – When you get back at someone for something they have done.

ACTIVITIES

Knowledge & Understanding

1 What does the Chaplain believe that God thinks about war?
2 Who started the just war theory 800 years ago?
3 From the following list, choose **two** statements which show why rules are a good thing in war:
  a They stop people fighting.
  b They stop arguments.
  c They stop wars escalating.
  d They make people fight fairly.
  e They stop people wanting to get revenge after the war.
  f They stop wars.
4 Choose one of the conditions for a just war. Explain what it means in your own words.
5 What do the Red Cross and Red Crescent try to do?
6 Match the following statements up with their moral stance (Christianity Islam Egoism Utilitarianism):
  a You should love your enemies.
  b Jihad means holy war.
  c Sometimes not going to war causes more suffering than going to war.
  d We just want to win the war – who cares how we do it?
  e Rules stop people taking revenge.
  f War is good if you are fighting against evil.

Analysis

1 You work for the Army careers office. You need to recruit more chaplains. Design a poster to do this.
2 Get everyone in your class to write **one** rule that they think should be kept in a war. Display these in your classroom. Are there some rules which are more popular than others?
3 You are a soldier. Your commanding officer has told you to go out and set some land mines. You know these will kill civilians as well as soldiers. You are not happy about this. In pairs, talk this through. One of you should be the soldier, the other the commanding officer.
4 Work in a group of four. Each person should write **one** answer to this statement. Each person should write as if they were one of the following: a Christian, Muslim, Egoist or Utilitarian.
  'Forget about rules in war. Just win it however you can.'
  e.g. I am a Christian, here's what I think about this statement.

Evaluation

'The Chaplain helps killers. He should be ashamed of himself.'
Do you agree? Give at least **one** reason for your answer.

Assessment question

Outcome 2 (11) Give **one** reason why an Egoist might not want to have rules in war. Give **one** reason why a religious person might disagree with this Egoist.

Homework

Find out about the work of the Red Cross or Red Crescent. Write a short report in your workbook. You could use the internet to get information.

Extension work

1 When people have broken the rules about war, they can be charged with 'war crimes'. Find out about a recent war crimes trial. Who was charged? What were they charged with? How did they defend themselves? Were they found guilty or not? How were they punished?
2 Find out about the Geneva Convention. What rules about war are in it?

NUCLEAR WEAPONS

CASE STUDY

Scary people in space suits. Flashing lights. Flames. A traffic jam. Up ahead, 10 nuclear bombs in lorries. Suddenly, chasing lorries full of bombs isn't fun any more.

No, it wasn't the X-files. It was 12:30 on Tuesday 26 November 1999. It was the M77 motorway near Hamilton. There had been a crash. The lorries with the bombs had to get past it. They did. So I followed. I beat them to Stirling with seconds to spare.

Scottish CND Magazine (adapted)

JUST ANOTHER WEAPON?

Robert Oppenheimer was a scientist. He helped make the first **nuclear bomb**. When he watched it explode he said:

I have become death. The destroyer of worlds.

Nuclear bombs were dropped on Japan in the Second World War. After this, Albert Camus said:

Society has come to an important point. We have to decide how we use our scientific discoveries. We can use them well, or we can use them to destroy the whole world.

Some people thought dropping bombs on Japan was a good idea. At least it brought that war quickly to an end.

What are the moral problems about nuclear weapons?

- Are they just another weapon? Or are they special because they are so powerful?
- Should we have them to scare other countries?
- Is it ever right to use them?
- Should we get rid of them in case there is an accident?
- Do they cost too much?

In Scotland there are nuclear submarine bases. Scottish CND (Campaign for Nuclear **Disarmament**) is against them. They have been protesting about bombs being moved around the country in lorries.

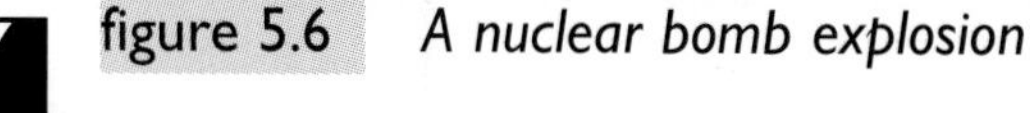

figure 5.6 *A nuclear bomb explosion*

DISCUSSION POINT

Is it right to have nuclear weapons?

In 1999, Scottish CND asked people 'Should Scotland have nuclear weapons?' The results were:

No = 85%

Yes = 15%

THE CASE AGAINST NUCLEAR WEAPONS

- When they explode they kill everyone around the explosion. They also have long-lasting effects. They harm all kinds of life.
- They are too big a responsibility. Humans are not smart enough to handle them.
- If one country has them, others will want them too.
- They could be fired by accident. A computer mistake is all it takes.
- They are expensive. Countries should do better things with their money.
- They are supposed to scare other countries so they do not fight wars. This doesn't happen.

Some people who are against nuclear weapons are against all war. Others are only against nuclear weapons. This is because nuclear weapons are so powerful.

When wars are over you want life to return to normal. That is difficult after a nuclear war. The remains of nuclear explosions could have serious effects for life on earth. It could change the world's weather. It could mean that all humans are wiped out.

THE CASE FOR NUCLEAR WEAPONS

- They are here. We cannot get rid of them. We just have to live with them.
- A country won't attack another if it knows they will fire nuclear weapons back. So, the weapons keep the peace. They are a good **deterrent** (see page 108).
- It is no worse to kill with a nuclear weapon than with any other kind of weapon.
- All wars affect nature. Not just nuclear wars.
- Nuclear weapons cost a lot. But it is a price you have to pay.

Supporters say that if you can hit back hard, no one will attack you. They argue that having nuclear weapons keeps the peace.

DISCUSSION POINT

Do you think most people are for or against nuclear weapons?

figure 5.7 *Nuclear weapons in transit*

TAKING A STANCE

People who don't agree with nuclear weapons often protest. Organisations like CND do this. The British government could say that most people agree with nuclear weapons. This is because:

- There are not that many people in organisations like CND.
- Most people do not seem to bother about nuclear weapons when they are voting in elections.

But some politicians don't agree:

The big political parties say we haven't enough money to build hospitals. We haven't enough money to support our schools. We haven't enough money to give free fuel to pensioners. But every year they spend £1.5 billion on nuclear weapons.

Tommy Sheridan, MSP (adapted)

Other politicians think that Tommy is wrong:

No-one likes nuclear weapons. But what's the choice? If we don't have them other countries will just take advantage of us.

Anon

DISCUSSION POINT

What is Tommy Sheridan saying? Do you agree?

TREATIES AND AGREEMENTS

In 1968 some governments signed an agreement (**treaty**). This was called the nuclear **non-proliferation** treaty. They check this every five years to see if countries are sticking to it. The agreement tries to:

- Make sure countries who do not have nuclear weapons do not get them.
- Make sure countries who have nuclear weapons try to get rid of them.

Some countries don't have as many nuclear weapons now. But there are other countries who are just starting to get them.

FACTS AND FIGURES

- In 1989 there were 65,000 nuclear bombs in the world. There are now only about 41,000 (Worldwatch Institute).
- In January 2000, the Russian President made it easier for Russia to fire its weapons first.
- Back in 1931, Einstein, the famous scientist asked all other scientists not to help make weapons.

figure 5.8 *Decommissioned nuclear weapons*

MORAL RESPONSES

CHRISTIANITY

Most **Christians** think nuclear weapons are wrong. The Church of Scotland says:

- They are against the rules of the just war theory.
- They do not bring peace. They make governments more jumpy.
- They cost too much. Governments have better things to spend their money on.
- Making and selling weapons makes money. So you are getting rich because people are getting killed. That is wrong.

The Church of Scotland says:

The Church has always said that nuclear weapons are wrong. It's wrong to have them and it's definitely wrong to use them.

Some Christians do not agree. They think nuclear weapons are the best way to stop wars starting. The strong should support the weak. Maybe one good way to do this is with the **threat** of nuclear weapons.

ISLAM

Some **Muslims** think nuclear weapons are wrong because they kill anyone. Muslims think you should show mercy in a war. You cannot do this with a nuclear bomb. This is because you cannot control who it will kill. Nuclear bombs don't take prisoners.

Nuclear bombs are expensive. You should use this money to help the poor.

But some Muslims think nuclear weapons can be part of Jihad, and are just another weapon.

India and Pakistan have been testing nuclear bombs recently. This has worried some people. They think they might use them in a war against each other. A member of the Pakistani government said:

There is no such thing as a nuclear bomb for Muslims. This is a weapon to defend Pakistan. That's all.

EGOISM

An **Egoist** could look at nuclear weapons in two ways:

- They would not mind using nuclear weapons if they won the war. But they would not want to cause harm to themselves by using them. For an Egoist, a nuclear weapon is just the same as any other kind. If it helps you win, fine.
- If using nuclear weapons makes the other side use them too, that is bad.

Egoists would not mind their country having nuclear weapons. As long as it kept the peace. But they cost a lot. Maybe the government should use the money for other things. Nuclear weapons can also cause harm by accident. So they are dangerous too. This would make the Egoist not want to have them.

UTILITARIANISM

Utilitarians would not like nuclear war. It would not bring much happiness. The effects would last for a long time. All life on earth could be harmed.

But a Utilitarian could support nuclear weapons. If using them saved lives in the long run. If you used a nuclear weapon it might stop a war right away. This could save lives for years to come. If the war had gone on, many more people would have died. So using them may not kill as many people as not using them.

Utilitarians might worry about the safety of nuclear weapons. An accident could be very harmful.

They might not like the cost of nuclear weapons. You could use the money to feed the hungry and heal the sick.

KEY WORDS

Deterrent – Something which puts people off doing something else.

Disarmament – When a country gets rid of its weapons.

Non-proliferation – When you try to stop things spreading or increasing in number.

Nuclear weapon/bomb – A very powerful bomb which uses atomic power to cause a lot of damage.

Treaty – An agreement between countries.

ACTIVITIES

Knowledge & Understanding

1 What did Robert Oppenheimer say when he saw a nuclear explosion? Why do you think he said this?
2 What two things are Scottish CND against?
3 Here is a list of arguments 'for' and 'against' nuclear weapons. Match them up with the right viewpoint.
   a They harm all kinds of life.
   b They are a good deterrent.
   c They could be fired by accident.
   d They cost too much.
   e They are too big a responsibility for people to handle.
   f They are no worse than any other weapon.
4 What does Tommy Sheridan think the government should spend its money on instead of nuclear weapons?
5 Give **one** reason why a Christian might be against nuclear weapons.
6 Why might a Muslim be against nuclear weapons?

Analysis

1 You are the Prime Minister. You are about to fire nuclear weapons on another country. You want to explain why to your people. So, you go on TV.
Add your own points to this speech outline:

> Good evening people of Great Britain. As you know we have been at war with Antarctica for five years now. Many have died. I have decided tonight to fire three nuclear missiles at our enemy. I know some of you will be against this.
> You may say [write here what you think they might say].
> But I have thought about it long and hard. I have, three reasons why I have decided to do this terrible thing... and I know it is terrible. They are:
>
> 1
>
> 2
>
> 3 [write here what you think he might say].
>
> I know some of you will be very angry. But I am a leader. Leaders sometimes have to make difficult choices. Tonight I have done that. It was not easy. I hope you support me. I will understand those of you who do not. Good luck, and may your God go with you.

2 You are a police officer guarding Faslane nuclear submarine base. Your partner is a protester. Write down **three** things you might say to your partner about the protest. Write down **three** things they might say to you about why they are protesting.
3 Using the arguments in this section. Design a poster either for or against nuclear weapons.
4 You have just heard the Prime Minister's speech in Activity 1 on TV. You decide to e-mail him with your views as quickly as you can. Take **four** points of view – Muslim, Christian, Egoist and Utilitarian. In groups of four each of you should prepare your own e-mail. You have only four minutes to do it. Time yourself. Then read each other's e-mails.

Evaluation

Using nuclear weapons is wrong. Having nuclear weapons is right.
Do you agree? Give **one** reason for your answer.

Assessment question

Outcome 2 (11) You are a pilot. You are going to drop a bomb on an enemy's big city. You only discover it is a nuclear bomb at the last minute. What do you do? Write how you would explain your decision to your children when you get home that day.

Homework

Ask as many people as you can what they think of nuclear weapons. Be ready to tell your class what you find out.

Extension work

1. Make up your own questionnaire on nuclear weapons. Report your findings to your class.
2. In Japan, after the nuclear bombs were dropped at the end of the Second World War, survivors tried to explain what they felt through art or poetry.
   Imagine you are a survivor of a nuclear war. How might you explain to people how you feel after your experiences. Use artwork, poetry or drama to get your message across.

6 GENDER ISSUES

DEPENDENCE AND INDEPENDENCE

CASE STUDY

This is what a woman should learn: To look good for men. To win a man's respect. To make a man's life happy. These are her duties. This is what she should learn when she's young.

Jean Jacques Rousseau (1712-78) (adapted)

What is a typical woman like today? She has a good job and works hard. But she may have to give up work for a while when she has kids. This could hold her back. She still does most of the housework. Male partners or husbands often work late. She does the ironing – hubby can't. No one's shown him how to. When she spends time with the kids she feels guilty. She's ignoring her work. When she works she feels guilty. She's ignoring the kids. She's the 21st-century superwoman!

What's new?

Are women's lives better today? In the past, almost all women stayed at home. During the First World War they took over men's jobs. The men were away fighting. Women showed they could do 'men's' jobs. Things were never the same again. Almost every job in Britain has been done by a woman now. Some men stay at home and look after the kids. But many people still think women **depend** on men. Some men still like that ideas.

Do you think we live in a 'man's world'?

Prove it

The United Nations says that women are equal to men. You cannot treat a woman differently from a man just because she is a woman. This is called gender (or sex) **discrimination.** But this is sometimes hard to prove. Is it discrimination if a man prefers his wife to stay at home? Is it discrimination for employers to make things difficult for working mums? Is it discrimination to see half-naked women all over magazines and newspapers?

Women's equality is a human right

Hillary Clinton is now a US Senator. In 1995 she argued that:

figure 6.1 *Hillary Clinton*

As long as women are paid less, fed less, fed last. As long as they are not allowed to go to school, the whole human race won't improve itself.

Anita Roddick, who started the Body Shop has said that:

Women just want to be free to do anything men do. Things have got better for women. But until women can walk around without worrying about being attacked, they are not really free.

Do you think men and women are equals?

The Scottish Human Rights Centre fights for equal rights for women. The Scotland Act (2000) is a law. Part of it says that women should be treated equally to men. The Scottish Executive thinks women's rights are one of the most important things there can be.

HAUD YER WESSHT WUMMIN'

Some men still think women should depend on men. Why?

- It is better for a woman to stay at home. The children get looked after properly.
- It is more natural for women to stay at home. And it is more natural for men to go out to work.
- Boys are not taught to do housework. Girls should be.
- A man is in charge of the house. He makes the decisions.

SISTERS ARE DOIN' IT FOR THEMSELVES

Many women (and men) think these are silly arguments. They think women have a right to be **independent**.

- Depending on a man is like being a slave.
- Why is it any more right for a woman to stay at home than for a man to?
- Why should a woman have to 'fit in' to a man's world?
- Even if women are different to men, what is wrong with that? Just because women don't behave like men – so what?
- Boys and girls should be taught the same things. Why shouldn't a boy learn to do housework?
- What gives a man the right to be in charge of a family?

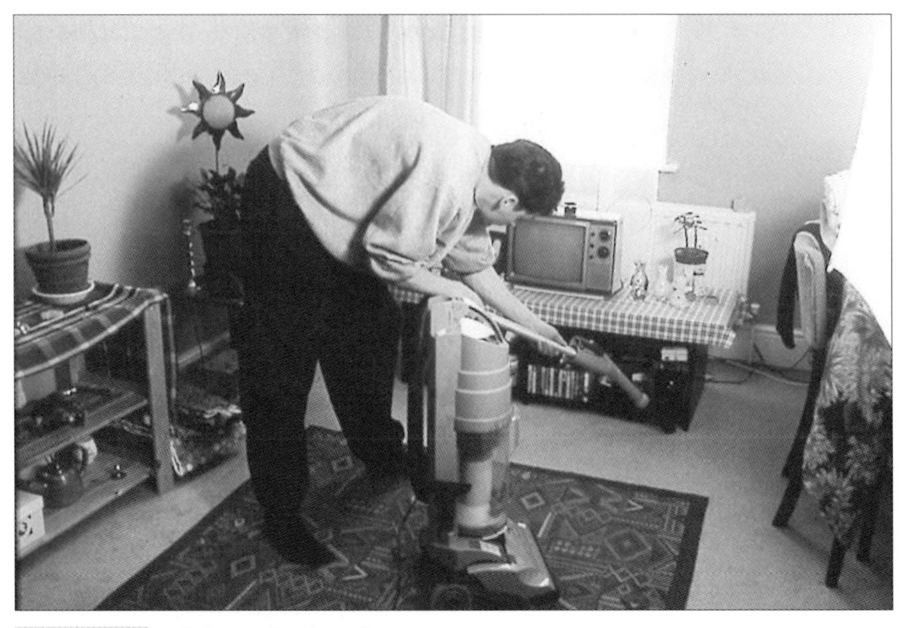

figure 6.2 *A househusband*

FEMINISM – REACTION OR REVOLUTION?

A **feminist** is someone who strongly supports equal rights for women. Feminists believe that men have put themselves in charge of the world. This is wrong and should be changed. In the past feminists have won the right for women to vote. They have also had success in other ways. Some women think feminists don't try as hard as they could nowadays. A famous feminist called Germaine Greer says that feminism is not only about equal rights at work. It is about the whole way men think of women. She says:

It is every woman's right to decide how she lives. The whole system needs to change.

MORAL RESPONSES

CHRISTIANITY

There is a group of **Christians** called Christians for Biblical Equality. They say that men and women are completely equal because:

- They are both made like God (Genesis 1:26–28).
- They both disobeyed God (Genesis 2:18).
- Jesus came to save everyone – men and women (John 1:12–13).
- Women can do the same jobs in church as men (Acts 2:17–18 and 21:9).

Christians think that men should be the heads of the family (Ephesians 5:21–33). But this does not mean they should lord it over women. It means men have special responsibilities. Husbands and wives should act as each other's servants.

Many Christians don't agree with women going out to work. Others say it is no worse than the man going out to work. God treats humans fairly. So men should treat women the same way. Women should not be dependent on men.

ISLAM

Muhammed was asked who you should obey. Three times he said, 'your mother'. Women are very important in Islam. Sometimes people say that **Muslim** women are not treated as equals. Many Muslim women think this is not true. They say that the rules about what women can and cannot do protect women.

The Qur'an says that women should be treated fairly. They can own things and spend their money however they want. Muhammed's own first wife was a wealthy women. In fact, she was his employer.

Surah 49:13 says that men and women are equal. Muslims show this equality in different ways.

EGOISM

If you are a man and an **Egoist** you might like working women. They bring money into the house.

A female Egoist might like being good at everything. But she might soon get tired of that.

Egoists would think equal rights for women are a great idea. If it makes life easier.

A male Egoist might like a woman who depended on him. Then he could boss her around. But he might not like it because then he would have to support her.

A woman might like depending on a man. If he goes out to work she can stay at home and enjoy her life. It means she can do what she wants. But then she might not be in charge of her life – because she depends on the money her husband makes.

UTILITARIANISM

The **Utilitarian**, John Stuart Mill, said that if women are not treated fairly, everyone suffers. He said that men should listen to women. He was saying this in 1869!

He said:

Men do not know much about women. They should listen to them and find out.

He said that society would only be really happy when men and women were equals. He said women should fight for their rights. He also said that men keep women beneath them. This stops everyone improving. This should stop. Men should not keep women down. They matter just as much.

So Utilitarians think that women should be equal to men. If not, society will not be happy.

KEY WORDS

Dependence – When you rely on someone else.

Discrimination – When you are not treated fairly.

Feminism – A way of thinking that believes women are equal to men in everything.

Gender – Whether you are male or female.

Independence – When you look after yourself.

ACTIVITIES

Knowledge & Understanding

1 Write **one** thing that Jean Jacques Rousseau said about a woman.

2 In Britain, when did women show they could do 'men's jobs'?

3 Here are some statements about women and equality:
- **a** It is more natural for a woman to stay at home.
- **b** What gives a man the right to be in charge of a family?
- **c** Women are better at looking after children.
- **d** A woman staying at home is like a slave.

Copy **one** which is for women being independent.
Copy **one** which is against women being independent.

4 Copy and complete, unscrambling the underlined words:
Feminists believe that <u>nem</u> have put themselves in <u>chrgea</u> of the world. This is <u>rwngo</u> and should be <u>chngeda</u>.

5 Which of the following statements are true and which are false?
- **a** Many Christians think that men should be the head of the family.
- **b** Jesus only came to save men.
- **c** Muhammed said you should only obey your father.
- **d** The Qur'an says that women should be treated fairly.
- **e** An Egoist would like equal rights for women if it made his life easier.
- **f** An Egoist woman would not want to be equal with a man.
- **g** John Stuart Mill said that if women are not treated fairly, everyone suffers.
- **h** John Stuart Mill said that society would only be happy when women were treated unfairly.

Analysis

1 Using some newspapers and magazines, design a poster about women in the 21st century. Show the different ways that women are portrayed.
For example:
Working women
Women in films and on TV
Women in sport
Important women
Family life

2 Find the female teachers in your school who have children. Ask them if anything is done to make their lives as working mums better. What more could be done?

3 Miss World is to be filmed where you live. Some people are protesting against it. Think of **three** arguments they might use. For each one, think of an opposite argument.
You could do this as a class debate.

4 The boss in an office has just said:
'Women shouldn't go out to work. They should stay at home and be good mothers.'
Split yourselves into groups, one for each of the moral stances. Think of **two** (polite) things to say to this boss.

Evaluation

'Women should stay at home. It is better for the children.'
Say whether you agree or not and give **one** reason for your answer.

Assessment question

Outcome 2 (11) 'Men should be in charge of the family.' What would an Egoist and a religious person say to this?

Homework

Design a questionnaire for working women. This should aim to find out how much housework a working woman still does compared to her male partner.

Extension work

1 Write a short letter to your local newspaper: 'Why men and women should be equals'.
2 Find **two** examples where boys and girls are treated differently in your school.
3 Make your own piece of artwork: 'Women: the right to be equal'.

OPPORTUNITY AT WORK

THE CLAIMS

Women's groups say that women get a bad deal at work.

- Women don't get paid as much as men. Even when they are doing the same job as men.

figure 6.3 *Equal Opportunities Commission poster*

- Women don't get promoted as far in their careers as men.
- There are still jobs that people think of as 'men's work'.
- Most women's jobs are still boring. Men get all the interesting jobs.

MEN ONLY

Do you agree that women are treated unfairly at work?

Why is this? Some women say it is because work is still ruled by men. They like to keep women 'in their place'. This is because some men think that women are 'weaker' than men. Why treat women as equals? This might make life harder for men!

Women's groups say that women are able to do any job a man can. If you look through history you will see.

I'M ALL FOR EQUALITY BUT...

Some men really think there are good reasons for being unfair to women at work. Here's what they say:

- Women are not physically as tough as men.
- Women can get pregnant. It is better for them to bring up kids.

figure 6.4 *Not equal or just different?*

- Women are too soft. Work is tough. Women are not up to it. They are not aggressive enough.

Many women think these beliefs are silly. This is what they think:

- There is no such thing as a typical woman. Some women are much tougher than men.
- Why shouldn't men bring up children?
- There are lots of aggressive women. It is just different to men's aggression (better!). Anyway, why can't you be gentle and still get on well at work?

Some men say that men and women are different. You cannot change that. As a result, work for men and women is different. Women say that things can change. It is the 21st century after all!

DISCUSSION POINT

Are there some jobs that should only be done by men?

FORBIDDEN TO WOMEN

There is one job that women are sometimes not allowed to do. In some Christian churches women cannot be ministers or priests. The Roman Catholic Church is completely against women priests. But there are women ministers in the Church of Scotland.

The Roman Catholic Church explains its view like this:

- It is not **traditional** for women to be priests. You should keep traditions.
- If you ditch one tradition, you might as well ditch them all.
- It is trendy to treat everyone as equal. The Church should not try to be trendy.
- Priests stand for Jesus. Jesus was a man. So a priest must be a man.
- Jesus did not choose women to be his disciples. He would not like the idea of women priests.
- Women can help in other ways. You do not have to be a priest to be a good Christian.

People who agree with having women priests say:

- Jesus had lots of women followers. He thought they were really important. He would like the idea of women priests.

- Priests stand for Jesus. But Jesus was more than a man. He stood for everyone. So a woman can stand for everyone too.
- Traditions should not be set in stone. They should move with the times. So should the church.

Should there be women priests?

Anyway, some women say it is not up to the Church. God chooses who he wants to be a priest. Why shouldn't he choose a woman? The Church says this is too simple. You could do anything and say 'God told me to do it'. This could cause lots of problems!

This is a poem written by a supporter of women priests.

How does your black waistcoat
Button me out of the Church?
Each button to be unfastened
Before I can creep in
through a button-hole
And hide in your handkerchief pocket
You fear me, and fasten yourself
neatly, tightly, up to the neck
So that I will not be your undoing.

Dancing on Mountains, Rev Flora Winfield

The Church teaches that there are no good reasons for women to become priests. We are not being unfair. It is God's plan.

Vatican Declaration, 1977 (adapted)

FACTS AND FIGURES

- Since 1977 there have been 12,344 cases of women saying that they are treated unfairly at work. The women have won in only 632 cases.
- In 1998 there were 18,700,000 working-age men in Britain. 15,700,000 had jobs. There were 17,100,000 working-age women. 12,200,000 had jobs.
- In the same year, 26% of women were doing secretarial jobs. Only 6% of men were doing the same.

figure 6.5 *A female Church of Scotland Minister*

MORAL RESPONSES

CHRISTIANITY

Most **Christians** believe that men and women are equals. God made everyone in his image. Everyone is free to choose what they want to do with their life. So, if a woman chooses to work, that is up to her. You should be treated the same as a man at work.

But some Christians worry about working mothers. They think this could harm family life. The Bible does not say that women are the only ones who can look after the home. But many Christians think so anyway.

Whether women should be priests is a big issue. The Bible can support either view.

For women priests: John 20:10–18; Galatians 3:26–8; Acts 2:17–18

Against women priests: I Timothy 2:8–14; I Corinthians 14:34–35

The question is, should Christians 'move with the times' or stick to the 'old ways'? Some think that only God can choose.

ISLAM

Muslims let women work. If they work they should be treated equally (Surah 2:228). There are lots of examples of Muslim women in positions of power.

Some Muslims do think a woman should stay at home. This is a way of protecting her. The family is the most important thing. If a woman stays at home then she has the most responsible job of all!

Muslims do not have priests in the same way as Christians. There are women who teach the faith. Some Muslims think this is wrong, because women should be protected from this kind of pressure.

EGOISM

An **Egoist** might have different ideas about working women. If you are a male Egoist you might like keeping women 'in their place'. This makes life easier for you. But if you have got a partner you might want her to work. This gets you more money. You will not be happy if she is paid less than the men who do the same job as her.

If you are a female Egoist you would want fair treatment at work. But you might also like to stay at home – if you think it is easier.

The same ideas would apply to women priests. It would depend on whether you are a male or female Egoist. It would depend on how much women priests would make your life better or not.

UTILITARIANISM

Utilitarians might be against working women if they thought this was bad for society. Maybe it is not fair that some families have two wage-earners while some have none.

A Utilitarian might say that stable families are important for everyone. A working mum might make this less possible. But then a man could do this job too. If a woman was forced to be at home, she might not be happy. This might make society as a whole less happy.

The happiest society is probably the one where men and women are treated equally in everything they do.

KEY WORDS

Opportunity – The chance to do something.

Traditional – Something which has been the way it is for a long time.

ACTIVITIES

Knowledge & Understanding

1 Some women believe that women get a 'bad deal' at work. Write **one** thing that they believe proves this.
2 Some men still think women should not be treated the same as men at work. Write **one** reason a man might give for this.
3 Anne believes that women should be priests. Margaret does not agree. Which of these things might each one say?

'You have to keep traditions – like men-only priests.'
'Jesus had lots of women followers.'
'Priests stand for Jesus so they should be men. Jesus was a man.'
'The Church should move with the times.'

4 Some Christians think women with children should stay at home. Why do they think this is right?
5 How do some Muslims think a woman can be 'protected'?
6 Would a female Egoist agree with women priests? What reason might she give?

Analysis

1 Design your own poster: 'Fair treatment for working women.'
2 Split into pairs, one boy, one girl. The girl wants to be a priest in the Roman Catholic Church. You must write an application for the job (even though you know you won't get it). Your application should look like this:

Dear

Application to be a priest from ____________________

I have thought carefully about this. I would like to be a priest. This is because [explain your personal reasons].

I know that the Church does not support the idea of women priests. I think this is wrong because [give your reasons here].

I hope you will think carefully about my application.

Yours sincerely

____

The boy is the person who receives the application at the Church. You must write back explaining what you think about women priests. Explain your own views, and the views of the Roman Catholic Church. You might make some suggestions about what the girl should do.

3 A sheet has been put up in your work place. On it, someone has written:

Working mums take up men's jobs

Each person in your class should write a response on the sheet. You should also try to put on the sheet what someone from each moral stance might say.

4 Look at figure 6.3. In groups, make a short video commercial encouraging people to: 'Prepare their daughter for working life'. You could take a positive approach.

Evaluation

'Priests stand for Jesus. He was a man. So priests must be men.'
Do you agree? Give **one** reason for your answer.

Assessment question

Outcome 3 (11) 'The Christian Church should move with the times or it will die.'
Give **one** argument for this statement and **one** against. Which one do you agree with and why do you agree with it?

Homework

Flora Winfield's poem supports women becoming priests. Write a poem which could be written by someone who disagrees with women priests.

Extension work

1 Design your own piece of artwork which either supports or opposes women becoming priests.
2 Write the words for a song which supports equal treatment of women at work.

VIOLENCE AGAINST WOMEN

CASE STUDY

Are you being abused?
Somebody close to you might be doing these things:
Hitting you. Threatening you. Forcing you to have sex. Abusing the children. Being nasty to you. Laughing at your views. Keeping you away from your family.
This could make you feel:
Scared. Embarrassed. Unable to think straight. Trapped.
If any of this is happening to you, it is domestic abuse.
You don't have to put up with it. It's not your fault.

North Ayrshire Women's Aid (adapted)

DOMESTIC VIOLENCE

Most of this happens in the home. One in ten women suffer domestic violence in Britain every year. One in four at some

figure 6.6 *Behind Closed Doors Campaign*

DISCUSSION POINT

Why do you think men hit women?

point in their life. But 64% of women that suffer don't do anything about it. Domestic violence happens in many different ways. Sometimes women are even raped by their partners.

VIEWS OF WOMEN

The charity Zero Tolerance was horrified to find out that many Scottish teenagers thought it was OK for a husband to hit his wife. Some people think domestic violence is partly caused by the way people 'see' women. Some men think they are above women. They think they are in charge of women. So they think it is all right to hit them.

A PERSONAL ISSUE OR A PROBLEM WITH SOCIETY?

Violence against women is wrong. It is an **abuse** of women by men. Why does it happen?

Personal issues

- Maybe some men are just violent anyway.
- Some men think it is a way of showing they are 'the boss'.
- Some women don't think they have any choice. They depend on their husbands to support them. But domestic violence happens to all kinds of women – even rich ones.
- Many women 'take it' to protect the children.
- Some women keep loving their partner. They hope he will change.

Social issues

- People don't want to get involved when a man hits his partner. They usually ignore it.
- Some men think women are there to be abused. Pornography on TV and in magazines might make men think this. It might make men think that women are things, not people.
- Sometimes men use violence to make themselves feel powerful. Most people agree that rapes are like this. They are not about sex. They are about power and control over women.
- Some men are brought up to think that the man is in charge. So some men might think they can keep charge in any way they like.

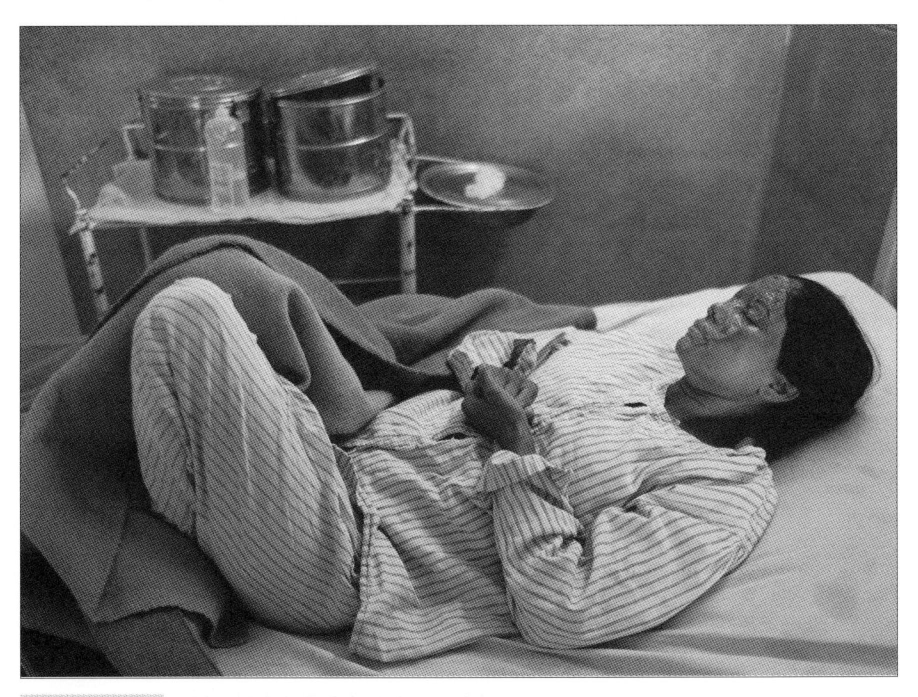

figure 6.7 *A victim of domestic violence*

Do you think society puts men first?

FACTS AND FIGURES

- A woman aged between 20 and 34 is most likely to be abused.
- Between February and November 1998, police in Scotland dealt with one case of domestic abuse every hour.
- About 1,155,600 adult American women have been raped by their husbands.

- Society works for men's benefit more than for women's. Violence against women is not always sorted out.

WHAT CAN BE DONE?

How can violence against women be stopped completely?

- Don't show women as weaklings on TV and in magazines.
- Have stricter rules about buying porn.
- Give harder punishments to men who are violent against women.
- Give more support to organisations which try to help women.
- Teach more about women's rights.
- Stop boys being bad to girls from nursery age.
- Give women equal say in everything.

CASE STUDY

Karen (not her real name) tells her story:

I married my husband in Glasgow in 1983. We both had good jobs. Soon he started to be nippy with me. Sometimes about nothing. This was usually after he'd had a wee drink.

Then we had a daughter. He was nice for a while. He had a hard job. He started drinking again. One night he hit me. I was shocked. Then he started to hit me a lot. He had a really bad temper. But he was nice to all our friends. One night I told him to get help. He really thumped me. I pretended I'd fallen down the stairs. I let him off with it.

One night he hit our daughter. That was it. We left. She's 12 now. She's not seen her dad since she was 8. I hope he never finds us.

figure 6.8 *A women's rights activist in Islamabad burns bed sheets taken from hospital beds on which two female victims died. Their injuries were burns-related, and they were caused by domestic violence*

MORAL RESPONSES

CHRISTIANITY

Christians are against violence. They should turn the other cheek (Matthew 5:39). But that does not mean a woman should take abuse. Christians think a man should care for his wife.

Some Christians think men are in charge. But that means they should still treat their wives well. Jesus always showed kindness to women.

Paul's ideas about women are mixed. But he says that women and men are equals (Galatians 3:28). He is quite clearly against violence against women:

Husbands, love your wives and do not be harsh with them.

Colossians 3:19

ISLAM

Muslims think men and women should be kind towards each other (Surah 30:21). The Qur'an says that men should protect women. But it also says:

As to those women on whose part you see ill conduct, admonish them (first), (next) refuse to share their beds (and last) beat them (lightly, if it is useful).

Surah 4:34

So, can a Muslim hit his wife if he wants to? Most Muslims don't think so because:

- Although this sounds harsh, it is a lot better than how things were for women before the Qur'an.
- Muslims say the Qur'an contains a lot more about treating women kindly.
- Men are in charge. But that is a responsibility – not an excuse to be nasty.

EGOISM

A male **Egoist** may have no problem with violence against women. But a female Egoist would. You do what is best for you.

But even an Egoist would have to think carefully. Your partner might hit you back. You might end up in jail. She might kill you. The courts might let her off because you were hitting her. Other people might treat you badly if they think you hit your partner.

When you weigh it all up, it is best not to abuse your partner.

UTILITARIANISM

Utilitarians would be against violence to women. It does not make society happy. If people put up with it, it would make life pretty horrible. What would they put up with next?

Violence against women could cause problems outside the home. It might make children more violent if they see violence. It might affect your work. It is in everyone's interest to put an end to violence against women.

KEY WORDS

Abuse – When one person behaves very badly towards another.

Domestic violence – Violence in the home.

ACTIVITIES

Knowledge & Understanding

1 North Ayrshire Women's Aid explains what abuse can mean. Write **two** of the things this can be.

2 What did Zero Tolerance find out about Scottish teenagers? Why is this worrying?

3 Copy and complete the sentences. Use these words:

things power involved the boss people control

Violence against women is wrong. There is no excuse. Why does it happen?

Some men think it is a way to show that they are t__ b__.

People in society let it happen. They don't want to get i____e__.

Pornography on TV might make men think women are th__, not __eo____.

Abuse is about po____ and c______ol.

4 Write down **two** suggestions about how to stop violence against women.

5 Reorganise this quote from Colossians 3:19 so it makes sense:

love Husbands, wives and your them be not harsh do with.

6 Even an Egoist might disagree with violence against women. Why?

Analysis

1 Make up a short information leaflet about violence against women.

Follow this format:

Page 1 – Artwork to catch people's attention. [Be sensitive about this issue]

Page 2 – Explain what domestic violence is. Put some facts and figures here.

Page 3 – Give some suggestions about how to stop domestic violence.

2 Imagine you are a member of the Scottish Executive. Draw up a list of things you could do to put an end to domestic violence.

3 'Karen' chose to leave her abusive husband. Write one statement that each of the moral stances might make *supporting* what she has done.

4 Design your own poster: 'Violence against women – there's no excuse.'

Evaluation

'The best way to end violence against women is to have tougher jail sentences for the men who do it.' Do you agree? Give **one** reason for your answer.

Assessment question

Outcome 2 (11) Give **two** reasons why an Egoist and a religious person would say that violence against women is wrong.

Homework

Find **one** example from a newspaper or magazine (or on a TV programme you have watched) which might make men think they can treat women as 'things, not people'. Explain what you have found to your class. Perhaps you could write to the newspaper or magazine.

Extension work

1 Prepare a short two-minute speech for your class: 'Why violence against women must end. Now'.

2 Your local church has asked you to design a stained-glass window. This window is to be for the 'silent sufferers of domestic violence'. Draw a possible design for this window.

7 ECOLOGY AND ENVIRONMENT

THE TREATMENT OF ANIMALS

CASE STUDY

I was sitting beside a huge female ape. Then I was really shocked. She pressed some buttons on a keyboard. A computerised voice came from the keyboard. It said: 'Has the visitor brought me something?' Bill, who works at the Georgia State University Language Research Centre, helped me. 'Yes she has. She's brought you some food'. The ape's computer answered: 'Good'.

Julie Cohen talking to Panbanisha, a 14 year-old pygmy chimpanzee, *Geographical Magazine* (amended), May 2000, p58

figure 7.1 *Sue Savage communicating with Panbanisha*

WHAT RIGHTS?

Julie Cohen says we should think again about animal rights. There is now a course in animal rights law at Harvard, one of the best universities in the world.

In New Zealand, it is now against the law to use apes in experiments.

In Britain, there are about 200 laws which deal with how we treat animals. These laws are often ignored.

Animals cannot always tell us what they want. So we have to decide what rights they should have. There are different views:

- Animals should not have any rights. They don't understand what rights are. So they shouldn't have any.
- Animals should have some rights. They are living things. So they deserve some rights.
- Animals should have the same rights as humans. Humans are animals. What makes us so special?
- Different animals should have different rights. Maybe the rights of a horse should be different to the rights of a fly.

Here are some reasons why animals should (or should not) have rights.

- Animals are worth something in themselves. This is called **intrinsic value.**
- Animals can be worth something to us. This is because they are useful to us. This is called **instrumental value.**
- Humans should protect the weak. Animals are 'weak'. This is because they cannot tell us what they want.
- If we care for animals, we will be more likely to care for people.
- Humans have always used animals as they want to. Why change that now?
- Humans come first, not animals.

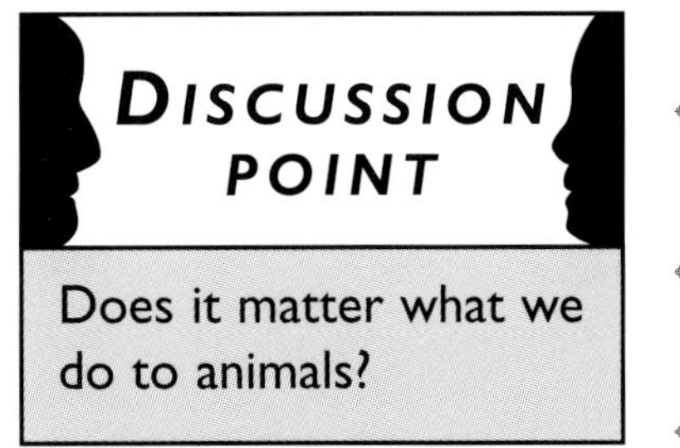

Does it matter what we do to animals?

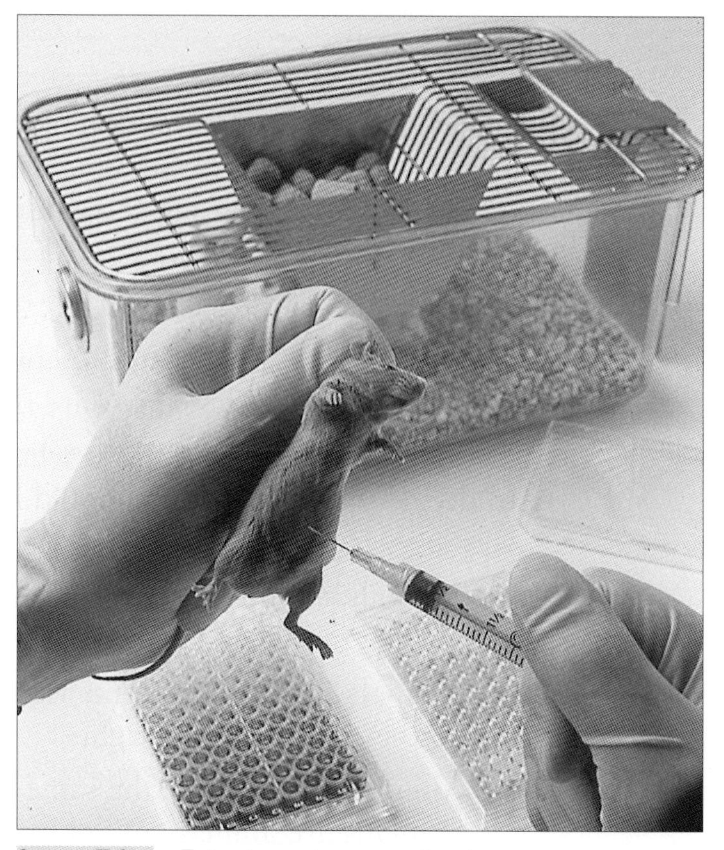

figure 7.2 *Experimenting on animals*

ANIMAL RIGHTS ISSUES

Animals as food

Arguments for:

- It is natural to eat meat.
- We have to eat meat to survive.
- Producing animals for meat is not really all that cruel.
- Animals eat each other – why shouldn't we eat them?

Arguments against:

- Humans don't really need to eat meat.
- Producing animals for meat is cruel. So is killing them.
- Eating meat is wasteful.
- It is the strong taking advantage of the weak.

Hunting

Arguments for:

- It has always been done (traditional).
- It protects farm animals from attacks by wild animals.

- It is natural.
- Sometimes hunting is the only way to get food.

Arguments against:

- It is cruel.
- You don't need to hunt for food any more.
- Because you have always done something does not make it right.

Cosmetic experiments (testing things like make-up and shampoos)

Arguments for:

- You need to make sure things are safe for people.
- It is the best way to test things. It is cheaper too.

Arguments against:

- There are other ways to test cosmetics.
- Animal tests don't always get the same results as they would on people.
- You don't need to keep doing it. Why do we need so many 'new' things?

Medical experiments (testing things like drugs and medicines)

DISCUSSION POINT

Do you think that humans are more important than animals?

Arguments for:

- You need to make sure drugs are safe for people.
- You cannot test a drug on someone if it might kill them.
- There is sometimes no other way to do the test.
- Only a few animals die. But they could save millions.
- Humans come first.

Arguments against:

- Drugs might be safe for animals but deadly for people.
- Why should humans come first?
- There are other ways to test things.
- Some tests are just for things like headache pills.

Zoos

Arguments for:

- They help protect animals which might go **extinct**.

- People can learn about animals. Then we will want to look after them more.
- Zoo animals have a good life.

Arguments against:

- Most zoo animals never get back to the wild. So zoos don't stop wild animals going extinct.
- People don't learn very much by watching animals in cages.
- Animals have a rotten life in a zoo.

Pets

Arguments for:

- They help us learn how to look after animals.
- They are good company.
- They have nicer lives than they would in the wild.

figure 7.3 *Younger member of a pro-hunting lobby protesting outside the Scottish Parliament*

- They do good things – like guide dogs for the blind.

Arguments against:

- Keeping a pet does not teach you anything. Apart from the fact that humans are in charge.
- Keeping pets in cages is not natural.
- Pets are sometimes kept just for us to have fun with.

DISCUSSION POINT

Should animals have rights? What rights?

THE BIG PICTURE

What would happen if we changed the way we treat animals? What if we gave them more rights? How would our own lives change? Should we give animals some rights, or full human rights? Could we work out a way to ask the animals? Or should we just leave things the way they are?

FACTS AND FIGURES

- In 1992, the SSPCA took 168 cases of animal cruelty to court. By 1999, this was down to 79.
- In 1997, the first successful case under new animal protection laws was won. Two youths pleaded guilty to using a hedgehog as a football.
- The SSPCA once got 31 people arrested and convicted for making dogs fight each other.

SSPCA Newsletter 8, Spring 2000

figure 7.4 *A sleeping brown bear in Edinburgh Zoo*

MORAL RESPONSES

CHRISTIANITY

The first **Christians** followed the Jewish rules about food. This meant they could eat some kinds of animals. But soon, Christians began to eat any kind of meat.

Jesus did not say much at all about animal rights. He did feed people fish. So he probably wasn't a vegetarian.

But Jesus did teach people to love others. He says we should treat them the way we want to be treated. Maybe we should do the same for animals?

Christians believe God put humans in charge of the earth. Maybe this means caring for animals.

But Christians think people come first. So you can use an animal to help people. You should not be cruel to the animal for no reason.

Aren't five sparrows sold for two pennies? Yet not one sparrow is forgotten by God.

Luke 12:6

ISLAM

Muslims have rules about food. They can eat some animals (halal). But they are not allowed to eat other animals (haram).

Muhammed said that when you were going to kill an animal you should do it quickly. You should not let it see the knife. This would just make it scared.

Muhammed said: 'Anyone who is kind to animals is kind to himself'. He didn't let his followers kill animals for fun. He didn't like people torturing animals.

Maybe this means that Muslims should be against experiments on animals? But if good comes out of it for people then perhaps that is good.

Muhammed said: 'If you kill a sparrow for nothing, God will ask you why you did it.' So Muslims think you should use animals when you have to. But you should not if you don't need to.

EGOISM

Egoists would not mind animals suffering if it was for the good of people. If a drug could save your life you would want it. You would not care if it was tested on animals or not.

You would want to make sure that you would not be harmed. For example, some meat is really cheap. This is because the animals are pumped full of chemicals to make them grow more quickly. These chemicals could harm people. You have to work out what is more important – cheap meat or your own safety.

Some people think that if you treat animals badly, it is easier to be bad to people too. If that is true, the Egoist would not be happy. He would want to make sure that animals were treated well. Then he has less chance of being treated badly.

UTILITARIANISM

Utilitarians would put up with some animal suffering if it was good for people in the long run. For example, a drug might be tested on animals. It might kill thousands of them. But this will help the scientists to get it right. Then the successful drug could save millions of human lives. So the testing on animals eventually brings good things – even though it is bad in the short term.

You have to weigh things up. It is not too bad if a few suffer so that far more get the benefit.

But some Utilitarians do not see it this way. They think that animal suffering is just as bad as human suffering. To cut this suffering down we would have to stop all the bad things we do to animals. This would mean a huge drop in suffering everywhere.

KEY WORDS

Cosmetic experiments – Testing how safe the chemicals in things like shampoo and hair gel are. This stops people getting harmed when they use the products.

Extinct – When a species dies out completely.

Instrumental value – The worth of something because it is useful.

Intrinsic value – The worth of something in itself.

Medical experiments – Testing whether drugs are safe to give to people.

ACTIVITIES

Knowledge & Understanding

1 Why is it so strange that Panabisha can 'speak'?
2 Copy and complete the sentences using the right phrases below:
different rights **same rights as humans** **some rights** **no rights**
  a Animals cannot understand rights. So they should have ____________.
  b Animals are still living things. So they should have ____________.
  c Humans are animals too. So animals should have the ____________.
  d Maybe different kinds of animal should have ____________.
3 Match the right phrase to the explanation.
Intrinsic value =
Instrumental value =
the worth of something in itself.
the worth of something because it is useful.
4 Choose **two** of the animal rights issues.
  a Copy **one** statement from each issue you agree with.
  b Copy **one** statement from each issue you don't agree with.
5 Why might a Christian feel it is OK to eat fish?
6 Copy and complete:
A Christian would not mind an animal being used in an experiment because....
An Egoist would not mind an animal being used in an experiment because....

Analysis

1 Imagine you and Panabisha could have a chat. This is what you might say. What do you think Panabisha would say back?
Copy this dialogue and fill in your own ideas:
You: *Well, Panabisha, what's good and bad about being a Chimpanzee?*
Panabisha:
You: *What do you think of people?*
Panabisha:
You: *What would you like most in the world?*
Panabisha:
You: *Would you like to be used in an experiment to help people?*
Panabisha:
You: *Why did you say that?*
Panabisha:
2 In groups of six, choose **one** of the animal rights issues.
Three of you design a poster based on one of the points **for** the issue.
Three of you design a poster based on one of the points **against** the issue.
3 Make up your own questionnaire on an animal rights issue. Try this out in your class or school. Report your findings to your class.
4 You are an Agony Auntie for a Christian Youth magazine. You get this letter. Write your reply.
Dear Auntie
I'm 14 and I'm a Christian. I want to be a vegetarian, because I think eating meat is cruel. My mum says Christians shouldn't be vegetarians. What should I do?

Evaluation

'Killing animals for food is totally wrong.'
Do you agree? Give at least **one** reason for your answer.

Assessment question

Outcome 3 (12) 'It is wrong to keep animals in zoos.' Give **two** arguments for this statement, and **two** arguments against it. Include your own views at the end.

Homework

Ask some members of your family what they think about some of the animal rights issues. Be ready to report your findings to the class.

Extension work

1 Someone designs a machine which can talk to animals. What would the animals say? Write this as a short story.
2 A zoo will be built in your town. Your friend e-mails you and asks you to join a protest against it. How would you reply?

DEPLETION OF RESOURCES

CASE STUDY

John Muir was born in Dunbar, East Lothian, in 1838. When he was 11 he went to live in America. He loved nature. When he grew up he became one of America's first **environmentalists**. This is someone who looks after nature. Environmentalists also try to make other people do the same. John thought that nature was good for your spirit. It was special. It was where people could find real happiness.

Others followed his ideas. They made the American government set up National Parks. All the living things in these would be protected.

The John Muir Trust works in Scotland today. It bought Ben Nevis. It wants to look after it. This means that people in the future will be able to enjoy it too.

John Muir said:

Everybody needs beauty and bread. Somewhere to play and somewhere to pray. Nature can heal. It can give strength to your body. It can give strength to your soul.

John Muir, *The Yosemite* (1912) p256 (adapted)

GIVE AND TAKE

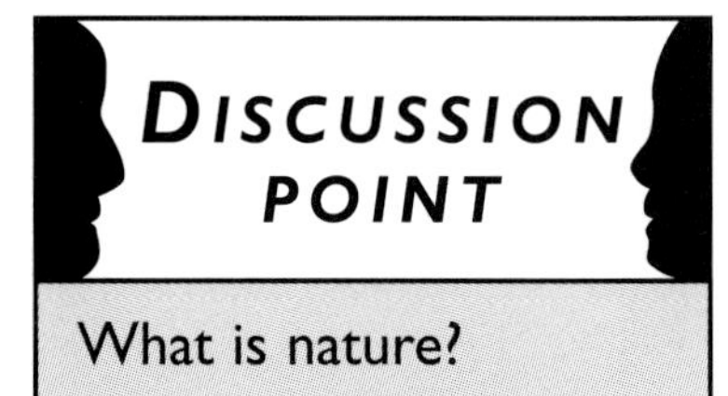

Humans need **natural resources** (things like oil, gas, wood, metals). Otherwise we couldn't make things. Are we sensible about how we use nature (nature is another word for the environment)? Do we give anything back? Or do we just take? What is nature anyway?

SHOULD NATURE HAVE RIGHTS?

Some people think that nature is a living thing. So it should have rights. Many religious people think nature belongs to God. So we should look after it.

If we are cruel to nature is it easier to be cruel to people?

Some think we should be kind to nature. If not, it might get us back. Or it might get back at our children. Maybe we should look after nature for our children's sake.

But is nature a thing? Can a thing have rights?

figure 7.5 *Statue of John Muir, Dunbar*

COMPARING THE PRINCIPLES

1 The environment is complicated. It is not easy to work out what an environmental problem is. It is not easy to know what to do about an environmental problem. We might make things worse.

1 We can't do nothing. We've got to learn about nature.

2 Nature can sort itself out. Even if it doesn't, humans are really smart. We can fix anything that goes wrong.

2 We have to be responsible. We need to use resources carefully (this is called **sustainable** living). Then they won't run out. Then there will be enough for everyone.

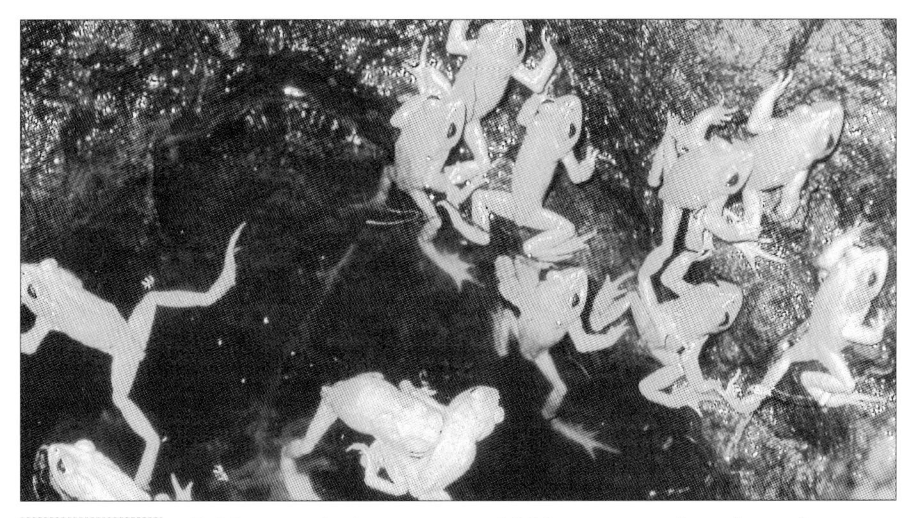

figure 7.6 *Golden toads, last seen in 1989, are now thought to be extinct. Scientists think this is because humans have damaged the environment in which the toads lived*

3 There are no environmental problems. There are just natural cycles. We just think they are problems. If we run out of something we can just use something else.

4 We have to survive. We have to use resources – as much as we need.

3 Humans have a big effect on the environment. We have changed it too much, too quickly. We need to do something. We have got to put it right.

4 Yes, we have to survive. But we don't need to kill everything else off.

Use or abuse?

Humans need to survive. We need to use natural resources. But sometimes what is best for us clashes with what is best for other living things.

- In China they are building a dam. It will be finished by 2009 and 1.9 million people will lose their homes because of it. Lots of land will be flooded. But the dam will bring people jobs.
- Scottish fishermen are sometimes not allowed to go fishing. This is to protect the amount of fish in the sea. It does not make life easy for the fishermen.
- On Harris in the outer Hebrides they are going to dig a giant hole. This will be used as a quarry. The rock will

be used to make roads. Environmentalists are against it. But lots of local people like the idea. It will bring jobs and money into the area.

- Scotland has lots of forests. But the trees were planted by people (they're called **managed** forests). They will be used to make things like paper and furniture. But this is killing Scotland's natural trees. This is because the managed forests take over the land where the natural forests would have been.
- Many people fight to save rainforests around the world. These rainforests are mostly in poor countries. Has anyone got the right to tell the poor countries that they should not use what they have? If they use the rainforest they can make people's lives better in their area.
- In September 2000 there were protests about the price of petrol. The government wants the price high. Then they think people will use less. This is better for the environment. But is it fair for people who need to use petrol?

figure 7.7 *Open-cast mining*

SPECIFIC ISSUES

Resource: Fossil fuels

Fossil fuels are made of prehistoric living things! These turn into chemicals which can be used to make energy. Oil and gas are examples of fossil fuels.

Problems:

- Burning fossil fuels causes gases. These gases harm the atmosphere. They are called **greenhouse gases.**
- Fossil fuels will eventually run out. Once we use them all up we cannot replace them.

Difficulties:

- Lots of people have jobs which are linked to fossil fuels, like miners. If we stop using fossil fuels they will lose their jobs.
- If we didn't use fossil fuels we would need other kinds of energy. These might harm the environment just as much.

Resource: Raw materials – metals, minerals etc

Raw materials come from nature. To make iron we need to mine rocks which contain iron.

Problems:

- Mining and quarrying for raw materials can harm the environment.
- The stuff which is left over when getting raw materials (**by-products**) can cause pollution.
- Raw materials cannot last forever.

Difficulties:

- Sometimes there is no choice. You have to use some raw materials.
- People's jobs depend on raw materials.

Resource: Organic *materials – wood, plants etc*

Problems:

- Getting hold of organic material can harm the environment.
- It might harm the other living things who need organic materials.

FACTS AND FIGURES

◆ In Europe we use 500% more drinking water today than we did in 1950.

◆ If we use 5% more fossil fuels every year there will be none left by 2047 (David Bellamy).

◆ Changes to the atmosphere have made the River Clyde double its flow (Dundee University).

- It could cause changes to the atmosphere.

Difficulties:

- When you chop down a forest and sell it you make money. But the people nearest the forest do not always get very much of the money.
- Sometimes there is no choice – wood only grows on trees!

Resources: Food stocks – fish, crops etc

Problems:

- If you eat all of one species, that can harm other species. So, if humans ate every cod in the sea, the other animals who eat cod would die.

Difficulties:

- Humans need to eat.
- The more people there are, the more food we need.
- People's jobs depend on things like fishing.

Most of the earth's resources cannot last forever. Using them might cause harm. We may not be able to work out exactly what the damage will be! Maybe we should follow John Muir's ideas. Or maybe we should hope we are clever enough to fix any mess we make.

MORAL RESPONSES

CHRISTIANITY

Christians think that God put humans in charge of nature. Being in charge is called *dominion* (Genesis 1:28). This means we can use nature. But we have got to look after it too. Christians believe that nature belongs to God. So we should look after it for him. This makes us *stewards* – people who look after things. It looks like Christians should be careful about natural resources.

But Jesus had some mixed views. He thought we should care for nature. But he thought we should use it for our own good too. In Luke 6:1 he lets his followers break rules. They are allowed to eat corn on the holy sabbath day. So does he think nature is second to people? Jesus also helps the fishermen catch too many fish (Luke 5:1–11). Is he saying we should take what we want from nature?

Some Christians are worried about caring too much for nature. If we do, perhaps we won't be caring enough about God.

ISLAM

Muslims think that the earth belongs to Allah. Every Muslim will be judged by Allah. He will ask how the Muslim has treated nature. If you do anything you don't need to, Allah will not be happy.

Many Muslims live in desert lands. Water is very important. All should share it equally. This is because all are equal as far as Allah is concerned.

You should use nature, but not abuse it. It is Allah's – you should treat it well.

EGOISM

Egoists might want to look after nature. If they don't it might cause them problems. Egoists want a good life. If you use up everything now, your life in the future won't be good. Maybe you should cut back what you use now. Then it will still be there when you need it. At least, until you have died!

Using resources which are good for the environment might also be better. They might be cheaper. The Egoist would like that.

Getting some resources might be harmful – like pollution. The Egoist would not like this.

Nature can only have rights if it does not cause the Egoist any problems.

UTILITARIANISM

Utilitarians would want to balance things. You can use resources as long as it is best for most people. But if you use up the resources then in the future people won't have them. That means that the people today (the minority) get pleasure. But the people of the future (the majority) don't. That is the opposite of Utilitarianism.

Utilitarians would also worry about the side-effects of getting resources. Pollution can be harmful for lots of people. Is it worth it to get something like gold or silver?

Utilitarians would want most people to benefit. That would mean being sensible about how we use resources.

KEY WORDS

By-product – Something left over when you make something else.

Environmentalist – Someone who cares about nature and wants to look after it.

Greenhouse gases – Gases which may warm up the earth's atmosphere. This change in temperature could cause serious changes to life on earth.

Managed – Something which is controlled.

Natural resources – Things from nature that we use to make other things.

Organic – Something living.

Sustainable – Using something now in a way which means it will still be around for people in the future.

ACTIVITIES

Knowledge & Understanding

1 Who was John Muir?
2 Give an example of a natural resource.
3 Copy and complete the sentences use these words:
God living rights
Some people think that nature is a ______ thing. Other people think it belongs to ___. So it deserves ______.
4 'Sometimes what is best for humans clashes with what is best for other living things.' Explain, in your own words, what this statement means.
5 Why does the government want petrol prices to be high? Is this fair?
6 Match the words to the explanations:
Steward =
Dominion =
Judgement =
Being in charge of nature.
Looking after nature for God.
When Allah decides how good you have been.
7 Reorder this passage so it makes sense:
The Utilitarian people most want would to benefit. That being mean would sensible how about we use resources.

Analysis

1 Design a poster using the quote from John Muir in the case study on page 141.
2 The government has decided to let a company quarry in your area. But this will destroy a beautiful forest. Have a meeting in your class to discuss the issue. The following people should be there.
Robert the builder: *He needs the rock which the quarry will produce. Otherwise he will be out of a job.*
Jimmy the quarryman: *Obviously a new quarry is good news for him.*
Jean the shopkeeper: *A new quarry will bring lots of new customers to her corner shop.*
Ian the unemployed man: *He might get a job out of this.*
Karen the environmentalist: *She is against cutting down the forest.*
Mary the Forest Ranger: *She will lose her job.*
Ken and Joan: *They will lose their favourite place to walk together.*
Think of some more characters on either side. Have someone chair your meeting. You might like to get together to discuss your arguments first.

3 You are a fisher person. To save fish stocks you are not allowed to go fishing for three days a week. Write a letter to you MSP explaining why this is not good for you or your family.

4 The government has put petrol up by 75p per litre. Which of these statements could be from the moral stances you have looked at? Copy each statement under the right heading (each statement may go under more than one heading):

Christians Muslims Egoists Utilitarians

- This is a good way to look after God's creation.
- This isn't good for me – I don't want petrol to be dearer.
- If this is good for most people, then that's fine.
- How will this affect people in the future?
- This might harm people's jobs.
- Good, I like cycling – it will get more cars off the road.
- Allah wants us to use what he gives us sensibly.

Evaluation

'We should use the environment to make human life easier.'

Do you agree? Give **one** reason for your answer.

Assessment question

Outcome 1 (11) The quarry in Analysis question 2 is to go ahead.

What might a Christian, Muslim and Egoist have to say about it?

Homework

Find out about National Parks in Britain.

Where are they? What is and isn't allowed in them?

Extension work

1 John Muir believed that nature is good for your soul. Write a poem or short story which explores this idea.

2 The government has decided to ban car use for one day a week. This is to save energy. Write what you think would be good and bad about this. Do this in groups and see who can come up with the most ideas.

POLLUTION

CASE STUDY

Cases of serious water pollution have doubled in Scotland. Fifty thousand fish were killed in Loch Queich, Kinross. This might have been caused by chemicals from a swimming pool. They were poured down a drain. Then they got into the Loch.

Four hundred trout died in a burn. They were probably killed by sheep dip getting into the water.

The Herald, 22 October 1999 (adapted)

EVERYBODY'S DOING IT

Breathe in. Breathe out. You have just caused **pollution.** Your CO_2 is a greenhouse gas! Almost everything we do causes pollution. The earth can cope with it. But only if the pollution is gradual. Sometimes it is not so simple:

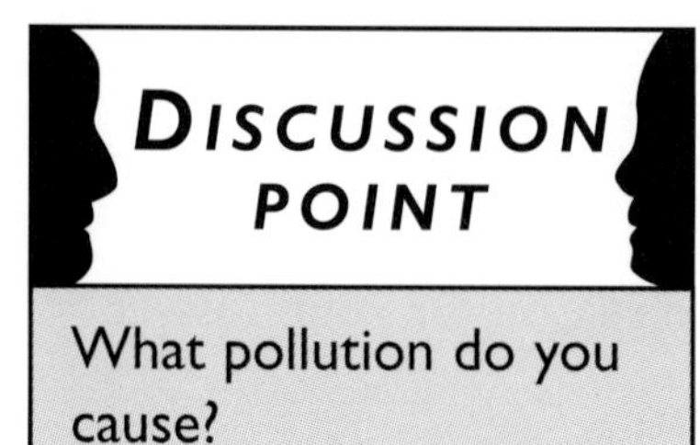

What pollution do you cause?

- Lots of pollution causes problems. Especially if it is in a small area.
- Some places are more easily harmed than others.
- Some pollution lasts longer. It causes more harm.

A GRADUAL PROBLEM

Environmentalists say that pollution has got worse. More factories. More farms. More fossil fuel use. All of these are to blame.

- Farms use more chemicals nowadays. These get into the water and the air. They can then harm people.
- Industry can cause pollution. Making batteries uses mercury. This is poisonous. Fossil fuels are burned. This creates harmful gases.
- Lots of things we do make **waste**. We have to do something with it. Some is buried. Some is dumped at sea. All of this can eventually harm nature. It can harm us too.

figure 7.8 *Pollution: this oil spill is a disaster for the local wildlife*

CASE STUDY

Friends of the Earth checked out 117 of Scotland's beaches. 25 of them were very dangerous. The water had dangerous bugs in it. Many were in an 'unacceptable' state.

Friends of the Earth Scotland

CASE STUDY

Winds from Eastern Europe are causing problems in Scotland. They are bringing pollution from Eastern European factories. But the car is still the major problem. The City of Edinburgh Council said that gases from cars are where most pollution comes from.

The Herald, 2 December 1998 (adapted)

DISCUSSION POINT

Some people cause pollution on purpose. Why do you think they do this?

WHOOPS!

Usually the worst kind of pollution is caused by accident. Oil spills from tankers cause serious damage. This happens very quickly. Accidental pollution can be simple. It might be caused by a big company dumping dangerous chemicals. Or it might be you dropping litter.

SO WHAT?

Pollution can destroy whole living systems. It can get into our food. It could change the whole atmosphere. It can harm nature. Or eventually it can harm human life. Pollution could even end it all!

CASE STUDY

Fish farms in Scotland might be killing shellfish. The World Wide Fund for Nature (WWF) says that waste from salmon in fish farms is the problem. It poisons the sea. This kills the shellfish. Lots of people depend on the shellfish for their jobs.

Sunday Herald, 17 September 2000

figure 7.9 *Anti-pollution protest*

SURELY SOME MISTAKE?

Maybe we cannot avoid pollution.

- People need to be fed. Farmers need to keep up with technology. They need to use more chemicals.
- Industry makes life better for everyone. But it does cause pollution. It cannot be helped. Things are getting better though. Industry is much 'cleaner' than it used to be.
- Accidents happen. We just need to deal with them better.
- Some people will always cause pollution on purpose. You cannot let that stop the benefits.

In what ways has modern industry made life better?

A BALANCING ACT

You cannot stop pollution. You just have to keep it under control. How?

- Make farms and factories better. Then there won't be so much pollution.

FACTS AND FIGURES

- 30 out of 173 Lochs in Scotland are 'fair, poor or seriously polluted'.
- 4% of Scotland's coastal waters are 'sub-standard'.
- Almost 65% of Scotland's canals are 'polluted'.

Scottish Environmental Protection Agency, 2000

- Find better ways to deal with waste.
- Use more things that don't cause pollution.
- Don't do anything. Nature will sort it all out.

figure 7.10 *An example of sustainable energy*

MORAL RESPONSES

CHRISTIANITY

Christians think they should look after God's earth. Because of this they should not cause pollution. But Christians should put others first. This can confuse the Christian!

You will not cause pollution because it will harm other people

You will cause pollution (not on purpose), because it cannot be helped. If you want people to get the benefits of industry and farming, you will have to accept some pollution.

Christians want to protect nature. But they want to help people too. Helping people have good lives might lead to pollution. It is not easy to decide which is the most important.

ISLAM

Muslims think you should be careful with what Allah has given you. You should only do what you need to. If pollution is caused by being extravagant (or just being good to yourself) then that is wrong. The Muslim should only take from nature what he needs. You should not cause pollution for no reason.

Muslims should speak out against wrong. Pollution for no reason is wrong. You should speak out against it.

EGOISM

Egoists could have different views. If the Egoist thought pollution would harm him, he would be against it. Even if the harm was not obvious, like, for example, changes to the atmosphere.

Egoists may not care about pollution. As long as it was not near them.

Egoists might ignore pollution. They might want to use a car. Who cares if it causes pollution. The harm will only happen in the future. They will be dead by then anyway!

UTILITARIANISM

Utilitarians would want to balance the benefits and costs. Everything causes some kind of pollution. We have to decide which pollution is OK and which is not.

Industry and farming can make people's lives better. But they do cause some pollution. It is fine if the pollution is not too serious and the benefits are big enough.

You need to be careful. What we do now might cause pollution in the future. This might affect far more people than are alive today. Utilitarians would not like this. So we have to weigh it up. Benefits now versus costs in the future. For example, burning fossil fuels today might be good for every living person. But this could change the atmosphere and harm people for thousands of years to come. Far more people than are alive today. So the benefits are outweighed by the drawbacks.

KEY WORDS

Pollutant – Something which causes pollution.

Waste – Materials which are left over and not wanted.

ACTIVITIES

Knowledge & Understanding

1 How does your breathing cause pollution?
2 State **one** way that farms cause pollution.
3 State **one** way that factories cause pollution.
4 Copy and complete the following sentences, using the right ending. You should discuss the possible answers because maybe more than one could fit!
   a Oil spills are a serious kind of pollution. This is because...
   - they smell.
   - they don't look nice.
   - they happen very quickly in a small area.

   b Pollution is bad because...
   - it costs money.
   - it can harm nature and humans too.
   - it is a living thing.

   c Maybe we cannot avoid pollution because...
   - people like it.
   - the causes of pollution can also make life better.
   - people need jobs.

   d You can keep pollution under control by...
   - shouting at it.
   - finding better ways to deal with waste.
   - not doing anything at all.

5 Give **one** reason why a Christian or Muslim would be against pollution.
6 When might an Egoist 'not care about pollution'?

Analysis

1 Sometimes waste can be put to good use. Collect some waste materials (like old drinks cans, paper bags etc.). Have a competition in your class to see who can come up with the most interesting uses for these materials.
2 When your parents were young they probably took bottles back to the shop to get money back on them. This was a good way to make sure they didn't end up lying around. The bottles then got reused. In groups, think up some ways that we could cut down the amount of waste we produce.
3 Using magazine and newspaper articles, design a collage:
'Pollution: Causes and Effects'
4 Carry out an inspection of your school and/or local area. How much litter is there? What could be done to cut it down? Produce a list of ideas to give to your Head Teacher.
5 The boss in a chemical factory has asked his workers to 'accidentally' dump some dangerous chemicals in a river. Three of them go to see him, one at a time.
One is a religious person.
One is an Egoist.
One is a Utilitarian.
Write a short conversation that each one might have with the boss.

Evaluation

'You can't avoid pollution.'
Do you agree? Give **one** reason for your answer.

Assessment question

Outcome 3 (11) You are the captain of an oil tanker. The government has decided that no more oil will travel in tankers. Instead pipelines will be built under the sea. These will take oil directly to refineries. How would you explain to the government that tankers are better?

Homework

Using newspapers, magazines or the internet, find **one** example of pollution that has happened recently. Write about it in your workbook.

Extension work

1. Lots of pollution is caused by trying to make things cheaply. This is because people want cheap things. Write to some shops (e.g. supermarkets, clothes shops etc.) Tell them what you have been studying. Ask them what their company does to make sure their goods are produced without causing pollution.
2. Look up 'pollution' on the internet. Make a small information sheet about the sites you find using this checklist:

Website address: www.____________________

What the site contains:

____

____

____

____

____

Useful links:

____

____

8 Revision and Study Guide

Making moral decisions

This course is about right and wrong. It is about how we make decisions about difficult things. You might never have to worry about some of the things in this book. But it helps to think about them. Why?

- You have already got to make moral decisions. Life is full of choices. For example:

  Should I tell lies for my friend?

  Should I take drugs?

- In a few years you will be grown up. People your age will run things. You will have to live with your choices.
- You will have to choose the government. You will want to understand difficult issues.
- You might have to face some of the issues in this book.

Studying this course gives you the right 'tools' to make difficult decisions.

Learning outcomes

A Learning Outcome (LO) is simple. It means 'what you are able to do after you have learned something'.

To achieve an LO you have to go through several steps. Here is an example:

LO = The student should be able to saw a piece of wood.

Step 1 – Get a saw.

Step 2 – Learn sawing action.

Step 3 – Saw a piece of wood.

INTERMEDIATE 1 LEARNING OUTCOMES

This covers only religious authority and egoism.

Outcome 1

You should be able to explain what each moral stance means:

Religious authority means you follow what your faith teaches.

You should explain how a moral stance affects a decision:

A religious person would do... about euthanasia.

Outcome 2

You should be able to give **two** views on a topic. Each one will be linked to a different moral stance:

An Egoist might think... about capital punishment. But he could also think....

Outcome 3

You should be able to say what *you* think about a moral issue. You should be able to give **two** reasons for what you think:

I think sex before marriage is ....

I think this because ... and also ....

INTERMEDIATE 2 LEARNING OUTCOMES

This covers religious authority, Utilitarianism and Egoism.

Outcome 1

You should be able to explain each moral stance:

Egoism is about doing what is best for yourself....

You should be able to say how each moral stance affects what a person thinks:

A Utilitarian makes decisions based on....

Outcome 2

You should be able to link the moral stances to issues:

An Egoist would probably not agree with nuclear weapons because....

Outcome 3

You should be able to show that you know 'both sides' of an argument:

Embryo research is good because... but some people think it is wrong because...

You should also be able to give your own conclusion. This should have at least **two** reasons attached:

I think this about embryo research .... This is because .... It is also because....

ALL TOGETHER NOW

People doing Intermediate 1 and Intermediate 2 will probably be in the same class. You will do the same topics. Your assessments will be different. Your teacher will help you decide what to you go for.

AIM HIGH!

THE SKILLS

The skills in this course are the same as they have been in your R.E. class!

KNOWLEDGE

This means that you should be able to work out what matters in a topic and what doesn't. You should be able to work out the difference between a fact and opinion. Sometimes it is not easy! You should keep your information up to date. Things change quickly. Read the papers and watch the news. You could keep a file of newspaper cuttings on the topics you study.

UNDERSTANDING

This means mixing what you know with new things that you learn. It also means putting what you learn into practice. It is like piecing a jigsaw puzzle together.

Each new thing you learn can be added to the jigsaw puzzle to make a complete picture.

ANALYSIS

This means picking things apart, then putting them back together. By doing this you will really understand something.

EVALUATION

This is like putting arguments on a set of scales. You put all the arguments for something on one side and all the arguments against on the other side of the scales. You can give each bit of information a value which makes it either light or heavy. By doing this you decide which argument you agree with. Which set of arguments is 'heaviest'? You need to know what to put on the scales though.

CONCLUSION

This means being able to express your opinion on something. You have your facts and opinions, you understand them, and you've been able to analyse how they fit together. You can then weigh them up and 'announce' your result.

Once you have studied something you should have an opinion about it. It may be the same opinion you started with. But it should now be based on evidence and is not just plucked out of the air.

HOW DO WE LEARN?

When a baby is learning to walk it goes through stages. It crawls. It pulls itself up (then falls over). It takes one step. Then it takes two. When the baby is learning to talk it points to something and hears someone say the word. It tries it out. Eventually it gets the word right. Then it adds other words.

Step 1 – 'teddy!' (pointing)

Step 2 – 'Want teddy!'

Step 3 – 'Me want teddy!'

and so on until: 'Can you pass me my teddy please? Yes that one there, the one with the red ribbon round its neck.'

Throughout this learning process, the child is adding new information to old. It is working out how one bit links with the other. This is what you have got to do with your new information.

If you want to be a good footballer you have to do more than play the game. You have to work on your fitness. Read about the game. Analyse videos and so on. When you are learning new things, what kind of 'training' is best?

Gathering information

There are many sources of information. Newspapers, libraries, the internet, your teacher, TV programmes, films and TV Soaps. It doesn't have to be an 'R.E. programme'. Gather together as much information as you can on your topic, including different opinions.

Sorting the information

Organise it. Use a folder, polypockets, dividers. Sort the information into facts, opinions, for, against, history of the topic, recent developments. Make an index.

Processing the information

Read a newspaper article. Summarise five of the main points. Make diagrams out of your written notes. Make up quizzes for your class. Make up easy ways to remember things. Put yourself into different people's shoes, imagine you are a Christian, Muslim, Egoist, Utilitarian. Act out role plays. Write imaginary letters or reports about a topic.

Reviewing the information

Test yourself. Read work you have already done. Does it make sense? Answer questions again. Are your new answers better than your old ones? Pretend you are the teacher. Mark your friend's work and get them to mark yours. Explain why you have given them the mark you have and explain how they could have done better.

ASSESSMENT

Your teacher has 'Instruments of Assessment'. S/he may call them 'NABS'. These are questions with instructions for marking. These will be used by RMPS teachers all over Scotland.

At Intermediate 1 your answers to the questions should be about 100 words long.

At Intermediate 2 they should be about 200 words long.

It is not much really. You will find yourself trying to squeeze in a lot of what you know!

If you don't get it right the first time you get another chance.

Let's try some assessment questions.

ASSESSMENT QUESTIONS AND SAMPLE ANSWERS

> Remember: In real assessment, all three questions at each level would be on the same topic (e.g. human rights).
>
> These answers are to give you some variety!

Intermediate 1

Outcome 1

Question 1

Describe the two moral stances you have been studying and show how each one relates to the issue of caring for the environment

Religious Authority: People here base their moral decisions on the teachings of their religious leaders, as well as holy books and answers to prayers. For example, Muslims follow the teachings of the Qur'an first. In the Qur'an it says you should care for nature because it belongs to Allah. Also, you will be judged at the end of your life. If you have been careless about the environment you'll be punished.

good – varied explanation of what 'Religious Authority' mea

relates idea of judgement to caring for the environment

Egoism: Egoists base their moral decisions on what's best for them personally. An Egoist wouldn't really care how he treated the environment as long as what he did didn't cause him any problems. If he thought his actions would harm him (like if he made Global Warming worse by driving his car) he might change his ways.

good, two possible ways an Egoist could respond to environmental issues are identified

(128 words)

Outcome 2

Question 2

What viewpoints might Egoists and religious people have on the issue of embryo research? Explain how each viewpoint is related to its own moral stance.

An Egoist would support embryo research because using embryos could help scientists cure diseases. This would be good for the Egoist because he looks after his own interests first. If it meant he could be cured from some disease he'd support the use of embryos. But if he thought that such research was dangerous (for example actually causing genetic problems) he might not be so happy – especially if these problems could somehow harm him.

good, clearly sets out what egoism means

again, good variety shown of different possible Egoist responses

Christians believe that life is sacred. Some think it should never be taken because life begins at conception – so embryo research is always wrong. Others think that we sometimes have to take lives if that benefits people – so embryo research is a 'necessary evil'. All Christians think we should treat life carefully because it is God's gift to us.

(136 words)

good, links sacredness of life idea to this specific issue

Variety of Christian viewpoints examined

good – reference to what Christians have in common with reference to this issue

Outcome 3

Question 3

'Capital punishment should be brought back in Britain. It's the best way of making sure people do not commit serious crimes.'

Do you agree or disagree? Give reasons for your answer.

I disagree. In countries with capital punishment there are just as many murders as in countries where there's no capital punishment. It's also a very strange way to say that murder is wrong by murdering murderers. People should be punished, but no one has the right to take away someone else's life – including governments.

(54 words)

good clear statement of opinion

solid evidence used to back up opinion (Reason ①)

good clear & reasonable argument (Reason ②)

Additional reason given – pupil obviously understands the issue and has evaluated it well

Intermediate 2

Outcome 1

Question 1

a) Give a brief outline of the three moral stances you have studied.

b) Choose *two* of these stances and state how they might affect someone's attitude to voluntary euthanasia.

a) *People who are Egoists make their moral decisions based on their own self-interest. They put themselves first in other words. As far as they're concerned their moral choices in life are based on what's best for them.*

Clear explanatio[n] of what the stances are

Utilitarians try to make decisions which produce the most benefit for the most people. They try to produce as much happiness for as many people as possible, and also as little pain for as many people as possible.

Good variety of ideas about how religious people arrive at moral decisions

People who make their moral decisions based on religious authority follow the teachings of their holy books or listen to their holy leaders. They may also pray and hope to be told what's right and wrong 'directly' by their God.

(116 words)

b) *An Egoist would think that it's entirely up to him if he wants to opt for Euthanasia or not. He might decide that his life no longer has much quality and so he'd be better off dead. Also, if he was in pain, he'd want that to go away because pain isn't in his self-interest. If the only way to make it go away was to end his life he'd want that. Finally, an egoist might avoid suicide because it could be painful and go wrong, so he'd want to know that he could choose to die but be helped by a qualified doctor.*

good varied ideas about what 'self-inte[rest]' actually mea[ns]

A religious person would most likely not choose voluntary euthanasia – <u>although there are differences of opinion about this.</u> This is because he'll probably believe that life is a gift from God and so should be cherished. If he chooses to end his own life he <u>'rushes into God's presence uninvited',</u> meaning he makes a decision that only God should.

Has identifie[d] conflict <u>with</u> moral stance

good use of relevant quotation

(164 words)

Outcome 2

Question 2

Following recent scares about BSE, Colin the Christian, Eddie the Egoist and Euphemia the Utilitarian meet in the pub to discuss whether or not they should become vegetarians. How might each explain their own viewpoint?

relates self-interest to vegetarianism/ meat-eating

Eddie the Egoist would want to know how likely it was that he would get ill from eating meat. If he found out there was a high chance, then he might give it up. Eddie's only concern would be his own well-being, the animal's wouldn't matter. If you could convince Eddie that vegetarianism was safer, healthier, or cheaper for him then he might think about it – as long as he benefited.

clear statement about Egoism

Colin the Christian might say that eating meat wasn't what God intended. Only after the Fall were humans allowed to eat meat – but some Christians think this was just a temporary measure which people should 'grow out of'. Colin would also say that humans have a responsibility to care for all God's creatures because humans have dominion over them. Eating an animal is not a good way of caring for it, so Colin would probably become a vegetarian happily.

good use of 'technical vocabulary'

Euphemia would want to make sure that not eating meat would benefit the majority. For example, if you could show her that vegetarianism was better for the environment – and so everyone – then she might give up eating meat. Also, if meat eating was linked to serious illness (like BSE-CJD) then she would give up, because such illness would not produce the greatest happiness for people, but misery.

(221 words)

clear exposition of utilitarian reasons for action

Outcome 3

Question 3

"Keeping nuclear weapons is morally wrong."

How far do you agree?

good link to other ideas of study of war

Nuclear weapons kill indiscriminately, and so break the rules of a just war, which say that civilians should be protected. They also harm the environment, and their effects can last long after the bomb itself has been dropped, like after the bombing of Hiroshima. Also, spending money on nuclear weapons is money that should be spent feeding the poor and helping the sick. Nuclear weapons' production and storage is also dangerous – nuclear weapons have been transported on motorways across Scotland. If there was a road accident, the effects could be very serious.

good, a numbe of arguments briefly put

clear expanation of some reasons behind an anti-nuclear stance

On the other hand, some say that maybe having nuclear weapons is why we have had no major wars since the Second World War. Having them has been enough to make countries think again about acting aggressively. In fact, having them makes it more likely that they'll never be used, whereas not having them could actually cause a war as a country could use them knowing that it can't be hit back.

good explanati with supporting evidence

On balance, I think that having nuclear weapons is morally wrong, (but that we don't really have a choice. You can't un-invent them, so getting rid of them now would just cause more problems than it solved). (Also, an enemy country wouldn't use them against us if it knew that we could strike back in the same way – so they are a good <u>deterrent</u>.) (Finally, nuclear weapons are evil, but all weapons are in one way or another. Giving them up would just be pointless.)

Reason ①

Reason ②

good use of technical vocabulary

(249 words)

Reason ③

THE EXAM

By the time you sit the exam you will have:

- Finished lots of coursework.
- Done Unit Assessments.
- Finished a prelim exam.
- Done practice exam questions.

By the time you get to the exam you will have had a lot of practice. So, the exam should be easy for you.

You can still improve your grade though. How? **Exam technique** is the key.

The writer of this book has marked exams in RMPS for the SQA for many years. Here are some tips which might help you.

- **The marker is on your side.** Markers are teachers. They want you to do well. They will try to give you marks when they can. But you can help yourself.
- **Answer the question fully.** Don't waffle. Try to write what matters in your answer. You have got to convince someone you know what you are talking about. In only a 'few' words too.
- **When you state something, explain it if you need to.** Sometimes answers just end 'in the air.' They don't go as far as they could. Make sure that you are clear about what you mean.
- **Learn how to cope with 'examspeak'** (see below). There are 'rules' about exam answers. If you know these it will help you.
- **Give your answer a structure.** If your answer is all over the place it is hard for the marker. It is not easy to find the right bits in a messy structure. Work out what the question is 'looking for'. Then plan an answer.
- **Remember, it is an exam in RMPS.** This course tries to help you work out your own ideas. But you have to learn about other people's ideas too. You should show that you have. For example, you should know what a Christian would think even if you are not a Christian.

- **Back up your answers with what you have learned.** You have to show the marker that you have studied the course!
- **Watch how your work looks.** Be neat. Be clear. Don't use words you don't understand. Watch your spelling. Don't try to be 'smart'. It is easier for the marker to give you marks when it is clear what you are saying!
- **Re-read your answer.** You might be surprised at the the silly mistakes you've made (read this sentence again!).

SOME TYPICAL EXAMSPEAK IN RMPS

Religious, Moral and Philosophical Studies is like all subjects. It has its own way of doing things. Exam questions are no different. Here are some typical instructions in RMPS exam questions – and what they mean.

- **Describe or Outline:** This means you state the important bits of the issue. For example: *Describe two viewpoints which people might have about capital punishment.*

  Your answer could start like this: *Christians think that no one has the right to take anyone's life because....*

  Christians think that Capital Punishment is the right way to deal with murderers because....
- **Explain:** Go further than describe, by giving the reasons behind the statements based on the moral stances. For example: *Egoism is based on the idea of self-interest. This means.... Because of this, an Egoist might believe....*
- **Do you agree or disagree?** OR **Express a personal opinion about/on:** Say whether you do or not! You can even say you are not sure. As long as you give your reasons: *In my opinion.... I think this because....*
- **Give (or support your answer with) reasons** OR **Justify your opinion with:** Sometimes they tell you how many reasons. Stick to it. Make sure your reasons are clear. Make sure they are reasonable! Watch out for very extreme reasons. For example: *I think.... because....*
- **How far do you agree?** OR **To what extent?** You should show that you know 'both sides' of the argument. Then

you should explain what you think and why. For example:

Q *'Marriage is out of date.' How far do you agree?* Your answer could be structured like this: *Some people think... this is because.... Other people think... this is because... I think... this is because....*

- **Double-barrelled questions:** Some questions have two parts. Answer both. Maybe you could underline or highlight the question on the exam paper. This will remind you to answer both bits. So for example: *Describe the two moral stances you have been studying in relation to Human Rights.* [part 1] *Explain briefly why they are important in making moral decisions.* [part 2]

There are lots of books about passing exams. But here are two things you can boil them down to:

1 **Work hard all through your course.**

2 **Practice at every opportunity.**

Follow these and whatever you do, it should be a doddle.

Good Luck!